MOTOCROSS

First published in 2006 by Motorbooks, an imprint of MBI Publishing Company, Galtier Plaza, Suite 200, 380 Jackson Street, St. Paul, MN 55101-3885 USA

MBI Publishing Company titles are also available at discounts in bulk quantity for industrial or sales-promotional use. For details write to Special Sales Manager at MBI Publishing Company, Galtier Plaza, Suite 200, 380 Jackson Street, St. Paul, MN 55101-3885 USA

ISBN-13: 978-0-7603-2555-1
ISBN-10: 0-7603-2555-3

Editor: Lee Klancher
Designer: LeAnn Kuhlman

Printed in China

On the cover: Ricky Carmichael flies the No. 4 Suzuki. *Simon Cudby*

On the frontispiece: The sign at Glen Helen Raceway. *Joe Bonnello*

On the title pages: *Joe Bonnello*

On the back cover: *Simon Cudby & Joe Bonnello*

About the authors
Joe Bonnello is one of the most respected photographers in motocross. Back in the day he used to pilot a pink Bultaco, but nowadays he's best known for his work with natural light and his aversion to wearing pants.

Steve Casper has spent most of his motojournalism career as an editor at *3&4 Wheel Action* and *Dirt Wheels* magazines. His racing resumé includes motocross, TT, cross country, desert, and ice events. Steve is currently the communications director for the National Off-Highway Vehicle Conservation Council.

Simon Cudby shoots for a variety of magazines and manufacturers and is one of the leading motocross race photographers.

Contents

Introduction

always looked at the concept of a man riding a dirt bike as a direct parallel to the evolutionary struggle of life on earth. How is that? Well, the goal of many species as they progress and mold themselves throughout the ages, whether predator or prey, is to run faster, turn quicker, and jump higher than all the other creatures that share their habitat. When a man throws his leg over one of these amazing motorized two-wheeled creations he built, he suddenly becomes the *über*-human of the savannah, able to blitz over any type of terrain with the fastest, most agile animals on earth. Man is no longer the slowpoke of the grasslands, relegated to climbing trees whenever a tiger shows up, but a high-flying participant at the top of the food chain.

Of course, the very day the second man built his own dirt bike the real competition began. Today we can try to imagine these two unknown riders lining up on their smoking, noisy hulks, dressed in nothing more than denim and T-shirts, hitting the throttles and squirreling around a crude course to see who

would be first to reach the old oak tree. And thus, the sport of off-road motorcycle racing was born in that very first *proto*cross.

Since then, motocross racing has evolved into an enormously popular activity throughout the world, with a rich history of heroes and legends, classic races and tracks, epic battles and rivalries, and innovative bikes and equipment. The future of this extreme sport appears even brighter as record numbers of participants continue to sign up every year and hundreds of thousands of spectators line the fences at outdoor tracks and fill Supercross stadiums throughout North America, Europe, and Asia.

What was once considered a fringe sport in America just a few decades ago is now mainstream. Every year, motocross racing and freestyle get more coverage on TV, and most young boys in this country know who Ricky Carmichael, Bubba Stewart, and Travis Pastrana are. Heck, motocrossers and freestylers even have their own version of the Olympics with the ESPN Summer and Winter X Games. It didn't take long for television producers to discover how spectacular it is to see a no-footed back flip on a dirt bike or 30 riders flying into the first turn and then sailing over a triple jump like the Blue Angels in formation. Motocross magazines and wild freestyle DVDs currently abound, and a few full-length feature movies have even been made about the sport.

Motocross and Supercross have not only become legitimate sports in the eyes of much of the traditional "stick and ball" news media, but the riders themselves are universally bestowed with "the fittest athletes in the world" tag. This isn't surprising considering the fact that nearly every muscle in a rider's body gets a tremendous workout with each lap around the track. Some have described motocross racing as requiring the same amount of energy as bench pressing 100 pounds with both your arms and legs for 20 minutes straight. Incredible physical conditioning is as much a part of the sport as are riding skill and bravery.

Ernest Hemingway supposedly said, "There are but three true sports—bullfighting, mountain climbing, and motor-racing. The rest are merely games." Motocross really wasn't around when Hemingway wrote those words,

but my guess is he would have certainly included it under the heading of motor-racing.

The machines themselves have an interesting history, coming a long way from the early "scrambles" dirt bikes of the 1950s. In those days, the steel-framed dirt bikes typically were heavy beasts that had antiquated suspension that beat the rider mercilessly in the rough stuff. Current bikes are high-tech marvels that are significantly lighter, faster, and more capable, but the sport is just as brutal and demanding now as it was then.

An entire industry has developed around motocross, and many fortunes have been made over the last couple of decades—on everything from the fully staffed factory race teams, to the exhaust pipe manufacturers, to the professional helmet painters, to the guy who invented a trick new type of handlebar grip. Motocross isn't only a pastime for many, it's a way of life.

The excitement surrounding the sport of off-road motorcycle racing, motocross, and freestyle is currently at an all-time high, so come along and join us as we explore the history, the people, the machinery, and the legendary tracks and races of this spectacular sport.

Moto-Variants

Motocross

Conquering Terra Firma at Warp Speed

Contrary to what most people might think, the sport of motocross didn't originate in America. Motorcycle racing on rough closed courses over natural hilly terrain was essentially invented in Europe, and for several decades that's where all the big races and the best riders were. When America began its own AMA National professional motocross series in 1972, European riders still dominated many of the stateside events. Since then, the sport has taken a 180-degree turn to the point that American motocross riders are now the dominant force in the world.

The premier American motocross series today is the AMA Motocross Championship, which features a 12-race schedule at legendary outdoor tracks from California to Maryland, some of which see upwards of 30,000 spectators in a weekend. Unlike the original European motocross tracks, which were carved into all-natural terrain, today's courses utilize lots of difficult man-made obstacles such as triple jumps, tabletop jumps, and long whoop sections.

Previous spread: Getting a good launch off the starting gate is key to winning at motocross. Rev it up, dump the clutch, and full throttle it through the gears all the way to the first turn. *Simon Cudby*

Opposite: Motocross tracks begin the day groomed and smooth, but by the end of the day, treacherous ruts can form on the faces of jumps and in the turns. When two wheels suddenly find themselves in two different ruts, the rider is usually headed for a face plant. *Simon Cudby*

The format for a motocross race is relatively simple and hasn't changed much since the 1960s. Anywhere from 20 to 40 riders line up twice on race day for two motos, or races, each counting equally to determine an overall winner. The motos can be as short as 15 minutes or as a long as a grueling 40 minutes (try that in the middle of August!). At the end of the day, each rider's finishing positions are added up and the one with the lowest score wins. A rider can finish second in both motos but still take home the overall trophy if

Louisiana's Kevin Windham shows perfect form as he hammers around a loamy corner. Surprisingly, the championship MX riders are usually the ones who can go through the turns faster than anyone else, rather than being the top dogs on the jumps or straightaways. *Simon Cudby*

the moto winners finish lower than third in their other race. In the case of a tie in the score, the best finisher in the second moto wins. There are currently two primary classes in the AMA Motocross and Supercross Championship Series: the premier class for 250cc two-stroke and 450cc four-stroke machines, and the support class for 125cc two-stroke and 250cc four-stroke equipment.

Motocross tracks throughout the country range from bare-bones local tracks stuck out by the cement factory to beautiful courses with "Ansel Adams" backdrops, like the Mammoth Mountain MX in central California pictured here. *Simon Cudby*

Modern motocross machines are mechanical marvels and can withstand lots of pounding and abuse. Unlike the old days, there are surprisingly few mechanical breakdowns during a race. *Simon Cudby*

While motocross riders are busy activating levers with each hand and foot, they also must constantly shift their body weight on the bike. On long, fast start straights, the key is to have your weight over the rear wheel for maximum traction. *Simon Cudby*

Next page: Today's motocross riders routinely catch big air that would have had Evil Knievel shaking in his white boots. With modern dirt bikes boasting over 12 inches of suspension travel, landings are considerably smoother than what Evil would have encountered on his big, heavy street bikes. *Simon Cudby*

Motocross riders have been described as the most fit athletes in the world. Virtually every muscle in the body gets a workout during a moto. *Joe Bonnello*

The cooldown lap gives the winner a chance to take off his helmet and salute fans. Ricky Carmichael has just taken the checkers in the moist, treacherous sand of Southwick. *Simon Cudby*

Supercross

Stadium Racing Under the Lights

The modern sport of Supercross is an all-American invention that can trace its roots to the very first stadium race in 1972 at the Los Angeles Coliseum (although MX historians will remind us that several motocross races were held in stadiums in Europe in the late 1940s through the 1960s). An immediate hit with cycle-crazy Southern California fans, Supercross has seen nonstop growth over the last three decades, packing fans into football and baseball stadiums throughout the country. Supercross organizers magically transform the stadiums into racetracks by hauling in tons of moist dirt days before the race and sculpting it into a challenging, jump-filled course. There are so many jumps on some tracks that the riders find themselves airborne nearly as often as they're on the ground.

Because most of the stadiums in the northern climes are enclosed, events can be held in places like Minnesota in the middle of winter. The format for Supercross differs from motocross in that there are a series of heat races where the top finishers go directly to the main event. Then the riders who didn't move up from the heats are given two more chances to make the main event in a couple of semi-qualifiers followed by a last-chance qualifier (LCQ). Unlike outdoor motocross

Next spread: Fans whoop it up as a night of racing is set to begin at the 2005 Las Vegas Supercross round, the last one in the series. While most of the AMA Supercross events are held in covered, indoor stadiums, there are a few southern venues that still take place under the stars. *Simon Cudby*

events, where the races are timed, main events for the premier class in Supercross run for 20 laps before the checkers fall.

Both motocross and Supercross events are run nonstop with no yellow flags to bunch up the field like in NASCAR and Indy car racing. When a rider does have an accident, a "local yellow" flag is used to caution other riders about the downed rider ahead, warning them not to make any passes in that section of the track.

Chad Reed, Jeremy McGrath, and Ricky Carmichael celebrate on the Phoenix podium by showering each other with champagne. *Simon Cudby*

Chad Reed (22) and James Stewart (7) demonstrate some stylin' moves at the 2006 Phoenix round. During rider introduction laps, fans can be treated to some pretty cool whips. *Simon Cudby*

Television announcer David Bailey is a former Supercross champion. Fans love his "been there, done that" insights into the sport. *Simon Cudby*

The spotlight is on ironman racer Mike Larocco as the riders prepare for another Supercross battle royale. In just a few days the temporary track will be gone until next year. *Simon Cudby*

Some critics of Supercross say the riders spend too much time in the air. You won't hear that sentiment coming from the fans, though. *Simon Cudby*

James "Bubba" Stewart is the most exciting new Supercross superstar on the scene. Astute fans knew they were witnessing the beginning of greatness during his first event in the 125cc class at Anaheim 1 several years ago. *Simon Cudby*

Tricky moves and tight racing are typical scenes during a night of Supercross racing. Here Ricky Carmichael (4) nearly puts David Villumen (12) into the hay bales at the 2005 Las Vegas event. *Simon Cudby*

Racer X magazine editor Davey Coombs hangs out with Supercross announcer Erin Bates. Coombs is one of the most influential people in motocross. *Simon Cudby*

Ever the showman, Jeremy McGrath is still treating the crowds to his classic freestyle tricks—sometimes right in the middle of a race! *Simon Cudby*

What's it like to be the big winner in front of 60,000 screaming fans? Ask Ricky Carmichael; he's been there plenty of times. *Simon Cudby*

Freestyle

From Nac-Nacs to Backflips

Freestyle motocross, as its name implies, is a no-holds-barred, anything-goes jumping competition. FMX, as it is also known, is an American invention and the newest form of dirt bike competition, coming into play in the mid-1990s.

Most would agree that the seeds of freestyle motocross were sown by the antics of late-1980s Supercross riders like Danny "Magoo" Chandler, Guy Cooper, and Rick Johnson. They made names for themselves by showing off in the middle of a race with "Tail-whips," "Pancakes," and "No-Handers" off the jumps. At the time, fans, photographers, and TV viewers ate it up even though the tricks were pretty basic by today's standards. In the 1990s, superstar rider Jeremy McGrath took it to the next level, regularly performing his trademark "Can-Cans" and "Nac-Nacs," in

which he would step off to the side of his bike while airborne. His background in BMX freestyle was quite evident at the time.

Freestyle motocross didn't become a competitive event until some race organizers began running "jump-off" freestyle shows during intermissions. The winner typically went home with just a trophy. Eventually some promoters began putting together all-freestyle shows complete with cash purses. This coincided with the release of the groundbreaking *Crusty Demons of Dirt* freestyle video, and the sport went wild, with many riders setting their motocross racing careers aside to join the professional freestyle circuits. The tricks quickly became crazier as riders started doing things on a dirt bike that most would have thought impossible just a few years earlier.

Twenty years ago most people would have said this was a horrific motocross wreck. Nowadays, stunts like these are commonplace with motocross freestylers. *Simon Cudby*

The sport radically changed in 2002 when FMX rider Caleb Wyatt performed the first successful backflip on a 250cc dirt bike. Today, if a rider plans on winning a major freestyle competition, he'd better have at least one backflip in his routine since even the backflips now have dozens of variations.

Previous spread: All over the world folks are packing arenas when the freestyle cowboy show comes into town, like this huge event in Mexico City. Major freestyle tournaments, such as the made-for-TV Gravity Games and the Summer and Winter X Games, feature up to five or six big jumps where the riders perform their timed routines. *Simon Cudby*

Jeremy "Twitch" Stenberg was a gold medalist at the 2005 Summer X Games. He is part of a loose-knit group of freestylers known as the "Metal Mulisha."

Taking a cue from freestyle snow skiers, freestyle motocross riders spend many hours jumping into a foam pit before attempting to complete their first successful backflip on real jumps. Once they have the trick down, they usually pull it off with very few mishaps. *Simon Cudby*

Many freestyle riders have built a sort of a "bad boy" image for their fans. Motocross and trail riding purists tend to frown on this somewhat negative portrayal of dirt bikers, but the fans sure eat it up. *Simon Cudby*

Fan participation at freestyle shows is high since their cheers at the end of each rider's routine can tend to sway the judges marks. This rider plays it up for the Mexican crowd by donning a traditional wrestling mask. *Simon Cudby*

A rider tests out some of the launch ramps prior to an outdoor freestyle show inside a huge Mexican bullfighting arena. Incredibly, riders are now able to let go of their machines completely in midair, jump back in the saddle, and hit the downslope with a smooth landing. *Simon Cudby*

"Cowboy" Kenny Bertram is one of the more colorful veteran freestylers on the circuit. Like their racing cousins, freestylers enhance their winnings each season with sponsorships from riding gear companies, bike manufacturers, and aftermarket distributors. *Simon Cudby*

Opposite: Sky, dirt, sky—"Cowboy" Kenny sites in a landing spot while in the midst of a backflip. Backflip variations are constantly evolving, and no one knows just where this sport may be headed as far as radical tricks go. *Simon Cudby*

Off-Road

Survival of the Fittest

The term *off-road dirt bike racing* covers a wide variety of competitions and includes enduros, hare scrambles, cross-country, desert, and endurance racing. Styled more for the competitors than the spectators, the races aren't so much a handlebar-to-handlebar battle between riders, but a battle of survival against the terrain. Proponents of off-road racing claim that these kinds of events reflect the core of dirt bike riding, since the tracks mimic a typical day of trail riding. More dirt bike enthusiasts can probably relate to the stream crossings, hill climbs, and tight, twisty wooded trails found on a cross-country course than to the triple jumps and monster whoops of a Supercross track.

The history of these various types of dirt bike racing in America dates back further than motocross, and most of them trace their roots to the post–World War II years when street bikers first started to ride their machines in the dirt.

Enduros are run on a challenging route covering wooded trails and dirt roads. Riders are flagged off in one-minute intervals and follow a set of route instructions as they try to maintain a designated average speed. The ability to stay at that average speed, combined with the needed bike-handling skills, makes enduros a unique challenge.

Hare scrambles and cross-country events are actually quite similar to each other and are typically conducted on long, marked loop courses over rugged natural terrain. Events are run for a designated number of laps or length of time, typically two hours. Competitive riders not only need to be fast, but also physically fit enough to maintain a race pace for hours.

Desert and endurance races can be either point-to-point or run in big loops, and they typically last anywhere from less than a day to 24 hours or more. Riders take off at timed intervals and must hit several

Off-road racing legend Larry Roessler is a 10-time Baja 1,000 winner, 12-time Baja 500 winner (last two times in a car) and 10-time ISDE gold medalist (in addition to two silvers and one bronze) in 13 attempts. *Joe Bonnello*

checkpoints along the course to be scored, with the quickest overall time at the finish winning. Pit stops and quick field repairs become part of the strategy, and in many cases a team of several riders competes on one bike. The world-famous Paris to Dakar Rally takes nearly two weeks to complete (all the racers stop every night to rest) and is the ultimate trophy for endurance motorcycle racers.

Previous spread: Only in off-road events do you get to race alongside quiet shorelines. On the other hand, motocross and Supercross riders don't ever have to worry much about hitting a moose, either. *Simon Cudby*

Left: It's not uncommon to encounter a little snow while racing in one of the west's Hare and Hound races. Riding through snow is a lot like riding through mud: put your weight back and pin it! *Simon Cudby*

Right: Cross-country racing is most popular in the eastern half of the United States, as riders blaze through deep, dark wooded trails and encounter stream crossings, hillclimbs, rocks, and dust—kind of like a typical day of trail riding, except at break-neck speeds. *Simon Cudby*

The newest form of off-road competition is Endurocross, which first hit the scene in fall 2004. It was wildly popular from the start and is unique in that it utilizes super-tough obstacles, such as boulders, logs, sand, water pits, and giant truck tires within a stadium course. Watch for this form of racing to get even bigger in the future. *Joe Bonnello*

Honda's current Baja racing team consists of California riders Steve Hengeveld (pictured) and Johnny Campbell. The major endurance desert events require a big crew of support vehicles and mechanics to cross the finish line in one piece successfully. *Simon Cudby*

Right: Desert downhills can be quite treacherous, even if you're going slow. Imagine racing down this rocky incline. *Simon Cudby*

Next page spread: Long-distance off-road racers have to get used to performing their acrobatics with only lizards, snakes, and stink bugs as spectators. *Simon Cudby*

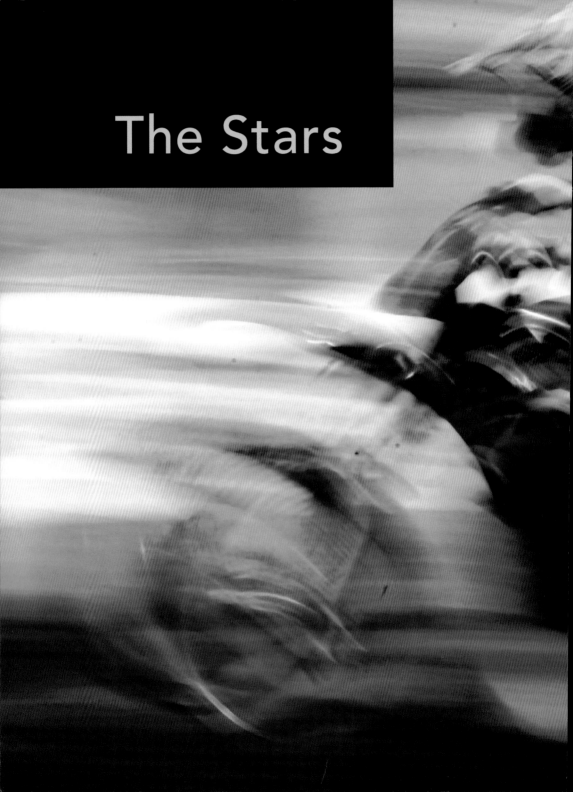

The Stars

Hometown: Clearwater, Florida
Nicknames: RC, GOAT (Greatest Of All Time)
Major Achievements:
AMA Pro Sports Athlete of the Year, 1996
AMA Pro Racing Motocross Rookie of the Year, 1996
AMA Pro Athlete of the Year, 2001, 2002, 2004
AMA 125cc National Motocross Champion, 1997, 1998, 1999
AMA 250cc National Motocross Champion, 2000, 2001, 2002, 2003, 2004
AMA 250cc Supercross Champion, 2001, 2002, 2003, 2005
AMA 125cc East Supercross Champion, 1998
Motocross des Nations winning team rider, 2000

If the sport of motocross were to end tomorrow, the name Ricky Carmichael would go down in the history books as the winningest rider of all time. Highlighted by two perfect seasons in the AMA Motocross Championship series in 2002 and 2003, Carmichael is still at the top of his game and is poised to solidify his domination of the record books even further. With four Supercross titles and nine Motocross Championships, Carmichael truly has earned the right to be called the GOAT—Greatest Of All Time.

Carmichael began riding and racing motorcycles at the age of five. As an amateur racer, he collected an amazing 67 championships. When he turned pro in 1996, Carmichael went on to dominate both AMA Supercross and Motocross like no other rider before him. To date, he is the all-time leader in wins in AMA Supercross/Motocross with a total of more than 130 victories. Since turning pro he has ridden for Kawasaki (1996–2001), Honda (2002–2004), and Suzuki (2005–2006).

When asked about his new competition from younger riders such as James Stewart, Carmichael says, "I think I'll always have a great reputation for winning a lot of races and championships, but unfortunately the nature of the sport is that you're only as good as your last race."

He also says he doesn't see himself racing motocross into his 30s like Mike Larocco and Jeremy McGrath. "I'd love to race NASCAR. After I retire from full-time motorcycle racing I'd like to keep doing select races. I'd like to do some GPs, Daytona, and a few Supercross or motocross races. Being around the fans is a great feeling. I'll probably end up flying by the seat of my pants and do some of the things that I sacrificed to get to where I am today."

The 5-foot 6-inch, 150-pound rider originally hails from Clearwater, Florida, and when he isn't testing or racing his Suzuki, Carmichael enjoys wakeboarding, hunting, and bicycling and is a fan of seven-time Tour de France winner Lance Armstrong.

No one in the world today can travel faster in the dirt on a motorcycle than Ricky Carmichael. He claims his determination is the secret to his success; his competitors would say there's more to it than that. *Simon Cudby*

Carmichael gets his race face ready before doing battle in the Motocross des Nations. He was on the winning team in 2000. *Simon Cudby*

Like all top motocross racers, Carmichael likes to unwind with a little trick riding on the practice track. *Joe Bonnello*

RC acknowledges the fans on a beautiful sunny day at the Motocross des Nations in Ernee, France. Every year, the MXdN is held at a different venue so no one country has home track advantage. *Simon Cudby*

Though the fans as a whole were a bit slow to start rooting for Carmichael (he was, after all, beating up on their hero, Jeremy McGrath), RC has now become quite popular wherever he goes. *Joe Bonnello*

Carmichael has won championships on three different brands of dirt bikes. In the early days of motocross when the technical aspects of the machinery were evolving at a much faster pace, the brand of bike seemed to matter more than it does today. *Joe Bonnello*

Hometown: Encinitas, California

Nicknames: Showtime, MC

Major Achievements:

Motorcycle Hall of Fame Inductee, 2003

AMA Pro Athlete of the Year, 1996

AMA 250cc National Motocross Champion, 1995

AMA 250cc Supercross Champion, 1993, 1994, 1995, 1996, 1998, 1999, 2000

AMA 125cc West Supercross Champion, 1991, 1992

Motocross des Nations winning team rider, 1993, 1996

Jeremy McGrath is easily the most popular motorcycle racer of the 1990s and perhaps in the history of the sport in the United States. A seven-time AMA Supercross and AMA 250cc National Motocross champion, McGrath's popularity transcends motorcycling. He has starred in national television commercials for a popular long distance telephone service, appeared on national network television shows such as NBC's *Tonight Show with Jay Leno*, and has been featured on countless magazine covers during his reign as the "King of Supercross." Video games, DVDs, toys, and collectibles featuring McGrath's name and likeness are among the bestsellers both within and outside the industry.

The sport of Supercross has grown rapidly, with much of that growth taking place during what many refer to as the "McGrath Era." With seven 250cc Supercross Championships, two 125cc Championships, one outdoor Motocross Championship, and two FIM World Supercross Championships, McGrath dominated Supercross like no other rider before

him and rewrote the record books. He also twice captured prestigious Motocross des Nations Championships as part of the U.S. teams, was the recipient of the AMA Pro Athlete of the Year Award in 1996, and has 102 AMA-sanctioned race wins to date.

Even though he became one of the greatest motocross riders of all time, Jeremy McGrath didn't work his way up through the minicycle ranks like most of his peers. McGrath learned his racetrack savvy and bike control while racing BMX bikes as a child and young teenager. *Simon Cudby*

His smooth riding style also included a signature jump he borrowed from the sport of BMX (bicycle motocross) and integrated into Supercross, the Nac-Nac (a backward Can-Can), which many feel helped spawn the freestyle motocross movement.

Even though he came to racing much later than most top motocross and Supercross riders, McGrath was able to translate many of the racing skills he'd learned in the world of BMX racing to motocross. After just three years racing as an amateur, McGrath made his AMA pro debut in 1989.

His utter domination of the competition became well known. During his reign atop the world of Supercross, attendance rose to new record levels, television ratings soared, and mainstream corporate sponsors quickly signed on. Most experts attribute the dramatic increase in the sport's popularity directly to McGrath. Beside his obvious racing skills, McGrath also had a mystique about him that gave him Hollywood-like star power, but he maintained the accessibility and genuine friendliness with his fans that has made him the most popular rider the sport has ever seen. Nearly every motocross rider who came to the pro ranks during the second half of the 1990s and the 2000s cited McGrath as his racing hero.

When asked about what he considered highlights of his career, McGrath cites his first AMA Supercross win in Anaheim in 1993 as the most memorable, but said that there were other stand-out moments as well. "I've had so many great races," he said. "My three Daytona wins were great because a lot of people said I couldn't do it. My outdoor national title was something people said I could never do."

Though retired from full-time Supercross and motocross competition, McGrath continues to fuel his racing desires competing in the Supermoto Series as well as occasional Supercross events. In October 2003, McGrath was inducted into the Motorcycle Hall of Fame. McGrath enjoys many outdoor sports—both snow- and waterskiing, wakeboarding, boating, BMX, and golf.

McGrath's racing career was marked by exceptional bike control; he rarely crashed. This kept him nearly injury free, allowing him to rack up championships year after year. *Simon Cudby*

Along with setting numerous win records for nearly a decade, MC was also a great spokesman for the sport of motocross. His off-track manner was always fan friendly, and Showtime never spoke ill of his competition. *Simon Cudby*

Another day at the office for Jeremy "Showtime" McGrath. Riding gear has come a long way since the days of Roger DeCoster. *Simon Cudby*

Most of today's top freestylers point to McGrath's tricks as being an early influence. Of course, when MC was doing Can-Cans and Nac-Nacs, there was no such thing as freestyle competitions; Jeremy simply performed the tricks in the middle of a race (usually while leading) as a bonus for the fans. *Simon Cudby*

Hometown: Haines City, Florida
Nickname: Bubba
Major Achievements:
  AMA Sports Motocross Horizon Award, 2001
  AMA Motocross Rookie of the Year, 2002
  AMA 125cc National Motocross Champion, 2002, 2004
  AMA 125cc West Supercross Champion, 2003
  AMA 125cc East Supercross Champion, 2004

James Stewart is not only one of the hottest motocross racers in the country right now, but he is also a pioneer. Stewart is the first African American rider to win a major motocross championship, and if his career keeps heading in the direction its currently going, he'll be an AMA Hall of Famer as well.

Known as Bubba to his many fans, Stewart entered his first race when he was four and was already a sponsored rider by age seven. He spent most of his youth traveling around the country with his family in a motor home, hitting as many motocross races as possible. Both he and his brother were home schooled on the road.

As an amateur racer, Stewart won nine national titles. He became known for his blazing speed and big air, which was unheard of for a rider of his young age. In 2002, Bubba turned pro and was named the AMA Motocross Rookie of the Year. His pro 125cc Supercross debut at the Anaheim opener was highly anticipated and, although he didn't win, most in attendance knew they were seeing the beginning of greatness.

In his first three professional seasons, the only rider who proved capable of defeating James Stewart was James Stewart. He was always spectacular and almost always the fastest rider on the track but sometimes fell prey to youthful exuberance and was injury prone. Nevertheless, by the time he reached his 19th birthday, Stewart had won two 125cc Supercross titles and two 125cc National Motocross championships.

Stewart is currently the biggest threat to Ricky Carmichael's dominance of the sport, and the record book on this immensely gifted rider has quite a ways to go before being completed.

He trains daily, riding on a Supercross track—complete with lights—in his 65-acre backyard in central Florida. Only a handful of riders have such quality racetracks at their own homes. (Carmichael, by the way, trains on a 100-acre personal training center about 20 minutes away from his home in Havana, Florida.)

"Every day I'm riding from 9:30 in the morning until about 4:00 in the afternoon," Stewart said. "I get a little break for lunch, but that's about it."

Hardcore motocross fans have long known about the little kid from Florida called "Bubba" and have been eagerly awaiting his entrance into the top levels of motocross. As we enter 2006, James Stewart has lived up to the expectations and is on the verge of being top dog in the country. *Simon Cudby*

One of Stewart's gifts is nearly unmatched corner speeds. Much like Carmichael did when he first came up to the 125 class, Stewart uses creative line choices and a blitzing, 100-percent style that isn't always 100 percent in control, but is faster than anyone else on the track. *Simon Cudby*

The cameras were focused on Stewart when he was only 9 years old. He dominated the mini scene at this time and was destined to be a factory pro rider. *Joe Bonnello*

Just past his 20th birthday, pitsiders have noticed a much more mature racer in Stewart. Rather than riding over his head as he did in his early pro career, he is now more calculating on the track and is content to stay near the front and let his competition make the mistakes. Here Bubba has a clear track at Southwick in 2005. *Simon Cudby*

In the 2003 season, Stewart specialized in the 125cc class and captured the West Supercross championship, as well as competing in the outdoor series. *Joe Bonnello*

In Stewart's quest to become national champion, he must first dethrone current king Ricky Carmichael. Three straight wins by Bubba at the beginning of the World/U.S. 2005–2006 Supercross season could get the job done. *Simon Cudby*

Like almost all athletes at the top of their profession, Stewart spends several hours every day practicing. In his care, that means carving turns and sailing over triple jumps. His current body fat index is about as low as it can get. *Simon Cudby*

Rick Johnson (left) and Jeff Ward (Wardy) are
two Southern California riders who achieved
motocross stardom in the 1980s. Johnson
amassed seven major AMA championships,
rode on four winning Motocross des Nations
teams, won four U.S Grand Prix events, and
was the first motocross rider to become a
two-time AMA Pro Athlete of the Year (1986
and 1987). Johnson could be described as a
pioneer of the freestyle craze, as he was one
of the first top riders to show off with tricks
over the finish line jumps. Ward was more the
quiet type who did all of his talking on the
track and became one of the greatest athletes
in AMA motocross history. Wardy has seven
national championships under his belt and is
the most successful American Motocross des
Nations rider, having participated on seven
winning teams. Wardy is still a top contender in
the AMA Supermoto championships and had
a fairly successful Indy car racing career,
nearly winning the Indy 500 on several
occasions. *Joe Bonnello*

In the motocross world, Belgian rider Roger DeCoster is simply known as "The Man." Five FIM 500cc World Championships and four AMA Trans-AMA Series Championship trophies grace his den. His influence on American motocross is immeasurable, as he first brought national attention to the sport with his mastery on the track in the early 1970s and then followed it with a highly successful career as team manager for the American Motocross des Nations team, Team Honda, and his current position as the bossman at Team Suzuki. DeCoster will go down in history as one of the sportís most influential and respected figures. Joe Bonnello

Bob "Hurricane" Hannah (center) was the most charismatic figure in American motocross in the late 1970s and ranks alongside Roger DeCoster and Jeremy McGrath as one of the sport's true icons. He was popular not only for his fearless, hang-on-for-dear-life riding style, but for his outspoken comments regarding his competition. *Paul Buckley*

Opposite: Bob Hannah's greatest years were from 1976 to 1979 when he racked up seven AMA championships, including three in Supercross and a hard-fought Trans-AMA title in 1978 that ended a four-year reign by DeCoster. His last major victory came in 1987 when he came out of semiretirement to help bring home the gold for Team USA in the Motocross des Nations that was being held in the United States that year. His inspired ride on that wet, muddy day was classic Hannah and goes down in history as one of the greatest moments in motocross. *Paul Buckley*

Mike Metzger is known as "The Godfather of Freestyle" and has been an influential part of the sport since it started taking off in 1997. He was one of the first MX freestylers to utilize foam pits as a training device. *Simon Cudby*

Opposite: Mainstream America gets a chance to see what those crazy dirt bikers are up to lately when the Winter and Summer X Games hit the tube. Here Metzger rips off a backflip from the snow jump in 2004. *Simon Cudby*

When you mention the words "freestyle motocross" to just about anyone, the first name that pops into their head is usually Travis Pastrana. The star of the Gravity Games and Summer and Winter X Games from day one, Pastrana regularly performs new and unbelievable stunts on his way to another gold medal. *Simon Cudby*

Opposite: When it comes to performing insane stunts for freestyle DVD crews, Pastrana is king. On this particular outing, Pastrana sailed off this cliff face on his motocross bike, separated from the machine in midair, and safely floated to terra firma with a parachute! *Joe Bonnello*

Pastrana's motocross career has had moments of brilliance, but has always been plagued with crashes and injuries. Lately, his interest has been leaning toward rally car racing rather than motocross, so the motorsports world may continue to hear from Pastrana for quite some time. *Joe Bonnello*

Opposite: If there's one person who can make backflips look routine, it's Travis Pastrana. In fact, the veteran championship freestyler recently became the first person to successfully pull off an amazing *double* backflip, but quickly retired that dangerous stunt from his repertoire. *Simon Cudby*

Ryan "Rhino" Hughes had been a longtime motocross and Supercross contender, but gained attention in 2004 when he won the inaugural Endurocross in Las Vegas. His win was quite impressive, as the field included top dogs from Supercross, enduro, desert, and Supermoto competitions. *Joe Bonnello*

Though Hughes has done of his most racing stateside over the last decade, he did compete in the European World Grand Prix motocross championship for several years. Here the California rider puts in a run at Mount Morris, Pennsylvania, in 1995. *Joe Bonnello*

Opposite: David Bailey, aka "The Little Professor," was known for his smooth, technical riding style and got his big break in 1982 when Roger DeCoster hired him to ride for Team Honda. He had a breakthrough season in 1983 when he won both the AMA 250cc Supercross and Motocross Championships. *Joe Bonnello*

Above: At the age of 25, Bailey's racing career was cut short after an accident at the beginning of the 1987 season. David refocused himself and became a world-caliber wheelchair athlete and an accomplished television broadcaster. *Paul Buckley*

Chad Reed won the richest Supercross race of the year in 2003, the U.S. Open in Las Vegas, and promptly donated much of his winnings to a friend who had been seriously injured while racing. *Simon Cudby*

Opposite: Australia's Chad Reed pounced on the opportunity to grab a Supercross championship for Yamaha in 2004 when the seemingly unbeatable Ricky Carmichael was out for the season with an injury. Reed never finished off the podium all season, racking up 10 wins in the 16-race series. *Joe Bonnello*

Oklahoma's Guy Cooper was well known as the guy who could throw his bike more sideways over the jumps than anyone else. He was also known as the fastest rider to never win a Supercross main event, but he does have a 1990 125cc outdoor championship to his credit. *Joe Bonnello*

Mark "The Bomber" Barnett was best known as a master of the 125cc class, but was also a 250cc Supercross champion, capturing the title in 1981 and nearly winning again in 1983. The midwestern rider's post-racing career is that of an expert track designer and builder for pro indoor and outdoor events. *Paul Buckley*

Below: This classic photograph captures Team Yamaha's Broc Glover sailing off a downhill at the 1988 USGP. In addition to his national championships, Glover also boasts the 1981 Trans-USA Series title, a pair of USGP victories, and a win with Team USA in the 1983 Motocross des Nations. *Joe Bonnello*

Above: San Diego's Broc Glover was tabbed the "Golden Boy" of motocross and actually took a few turns in front of the cameras for a couple of motocross movies. Fortunately for Glover, his racing career was much more successful than his stint as a movie star. Glover's six AMA outdoor national championships stood as a record for nearly 20 years, and he is one of only six riders to have won more than 50 major AMA victories. *Paul Buckley*

At the close of the 1994 season, Sherwood, Michigan's Jeff Stanton retired at age 26 among the AMA's all-time top-10 race winners. During the 1989–1992 seasons, Stanton was the nation's dominant motocross and Supercross rider while riding for the mighty Team Honda. *Joe Bonnello*

Along with his stateside victories, Jeff Stanton was also the FIM World Supercross Champion (1992) and on the winning Motocross des Nations team three times (1989–1991). Since then he's stayed very involved in the sport by serving as the rider's coach for Team Honda. *Paul Buckley*

Mike LaRocco is the most durable motocross star since Jeff Ward, and he has remained a solid top-five competitor into his mid-30s. Pictured here with his wife, Beth, the Indiana rider has two outdoor national championships to his credit, as well as an FIM World Supercross Championship in 2000. He was part of the Motocross des Nations winning teams in 1992 and 2000. *Joe Bonnello*

Mike LaRocco is arguably the best Supercross rider *not* to have won the AMA Supercross Championship. Prior to the 2006 season, he won 10 250cc main events, was runner-up in the series to Jeremy McGrath in 1994, and placed third in the series on four occasions. *Simon Cudby*

Louisiana native Kevin Windham has had an up-and-down motocross career marked by days where no one could touch him on the track, to complete seasons lost due to injuries. *Simon Cudby*

Opposite: Kevin "Kdub" Windham is currently a member of Team Honda and races the mighty CRF450R in both the Supercross and outdoor series. He's known for his fluid, smooth riding style and is relatively quiet off-track. *Simon Cudby*

Doug Henry got his start in the busy New England motocross scene and is a fan favorite not only for his race victories, but also for his amazing comebacks from two bouts of serious injury. As if breaking both wrists in one wreck wasn't enough to slow him down for a while, Henry accidentally sailed off a huge jump with too much throttle and broke his back. In both instances he worked his way back to winning form. *Joe Bonnello*

Opposite: Named the AMA 1998 Pro Athlete of the Year, Doug Henry can claim three outdoor national championships, as well as the 1993 East Supercross title to his name. During his career, Henry rode for both Yamaha and Honda. *Joe Bonnello*

Next page spread: Doug Henry was a pioneer, being one of the first racers to ride the big-bore four-strokes against the established 250cc two-stroke-powered machines. He also gave pro snowmobile Snocross racing a try in the late 1990s. *Joe Bonnello*

Jeff Emig's career took a downturn in 1998 and 1999 with a series of injuries and the loss of his factory Kawasaki ride. He returned to form briefly and won the 1999 U.S. Open in Las Vegas, but retired from pro racing after another injury in 2000. *Joe Bonnello*

Right: Rising from the mini ranks, Kansas City, Missouri, racer Jeff Emig scored four AMA National Championships: the 1992 125cc National Motocross Championship, back-to-back 250cc outdoor titles in 1996 and 1997, and the 1997 250cc Supercross Championship. His superb 1997 season earned him AMA Pro Athlete of the Year honors. *Joe Bonnello*

Jeff Emig had the unfortunate luck of having the peak years of his racing career coincide with Jeremy McGrath's. They locked horns many times throughout the 1990s, and even though McGrath dominated the era and became a superstar, Emig won his fair share. *Joe Bonnello*

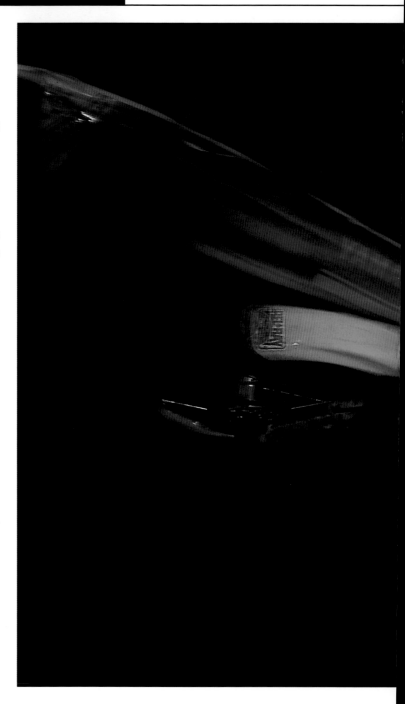

Other Names
You Should Know

Previous spread: Suzuki racer Broc Hepler was destined to be a motocrosser the day the nurse first wrote his name on his ankleband at the hospital. Hepler's dad was such a motocross fanatic that he named his newborn son after Broc Glover. Today Hepler rides for Team Makita Suzuki in both indoor and outdoor events. *Joe Bonnello*

Ivan "Hot Sauce" Tedesco is a native of New Mexico and can lay claim to the 2004 and 2005 125cc West Coast SX Championship, as well as the 2005 125cc Outdoor National Championship riding aboard a factory Suzuki A step up to the big-bike class is next on the agenda for this 24-year-old racer. *Simon Cudby*

Grant Langston honed his career in his native South Africa and was a World Grand Prix competitor at a record young age of 15 in 1998. Langston is now a U.S. resident and focuses on the AMA circuit, where he was the 2003 125cc Motocross Champion. Here he shakes himself off after a tough fall at Hangtown. *Simon Cudby*

No motocross racer has ever started his pro career with as much hoopla or controversy as teenager Mike Alessi. With coaching from his father, Tony, Alessi dominated the minicycle racing world all the way from his 50cc days and was a factory rider before he hit high school. By the time he was ready for the big show, Alessi's team was making motocross headlines by proclaiming victories and championships before the gates dropped. The debut at the Millville National didn't go as planned for the SoCal-based team, but the last chapter is far from being written on this determined and extremely talented racer. *Simon Cudby*

"I do this because I love riding my dirt bike," says freestyler Nate Adams. "There are too many hassles and there is too much danger in the sport to do it for any other reason. You have to love it enough to be willing to put your body, health, and in some circumstances your life on the line." *Simon Cudby*

Washington racer Ryan Villopoto lists skiing—water and snow—as two of his favorite non-motorized pastimes. Villopoto currently runs for Team Kawasaki. *Simon Cudby*

Below: A longtime Team Honda rider for endurance/desert events, Steve Hengeveld has also dabbled in the relatively new sport of Supermoto, where competitors race on tracks consisting of both pavement and dirt. In 2005 he was the SCORE National Champion as well as being the AMA Hare and Hound four-stroke champion. *Simon Cudby*

Left: Pro racer Josh Dement churns some heavy dirt as he chases the checkers aboard his Suzuki. Motocross racers have to be prepared for just about any weather situation that is thrown their way, including intense heat, rain, and sometimes even snow flurries. *Joe Bonnello*

Colorado racer Andrew Short's current claim to fame is sweeping the Bercy SX in 2004 when he won the main event three nights in a row in the stadium outside Paris, France. *Simon Cudby*

Tennessee native Mike Brown wears a mask of dirt after an especially tough run. Brown was the 2001 125cc AMA Motocross Champion and has two Labrador retrievers named Duke and Daisy. *Simon Cudby*

Veteran off-road racer Larry Roessler has won titles in just about every form of off-road motorcycle competition. His trophy case holds championship awards from desert, enduro, ISDE, Hare and Hound, and Grand Prix. In the last decade he has switched his allegiance to four wheels and has won several desert races in his off-road truck. *Joe Bonnello*

When Ezra "Yogi" Lusk isn't injured, the Georgia rider is tough to beat and has several Supercross wins to his credit. *Joe Bonnello*

Frenchman Sebastian Tortelli won a World Grand Prix Championship in 1998, came to the United States to contest the series here on a Suzuki, and has since returned to Europe for another go at the world title with his new KTM ride. *Joe Bonnello*

Left: Steve Lamson is a native of the Sacramento area and considers Hangtown his home event. Lamson held the 125cc National Champion title in 1995 and 1996 and is third on the list of all-time 125cc National winners, preceded only by Ricky Carmichael and Mark Barnett. In 1996, Lamson became the only rider to ever win the overall title at the Motocross des Nations in Jerez, Spain, on a 125cc racing against 250ccs and 500ccs. *Joe Bonnello*

Marty Tripes is known as one of the most naturally talented riders in motocross history. A top-ranked racer in the 1970s and early 1980s, his best-known victory came at the Superbowl of Motocross at the Los Angeles Coliseum in July 1972, just a few weeks after he turned 16. *Paul Buckley*

Below: Also known as "The Rhinestone Cowboy," Texan Kent Howerton lays claim to being the only rider to capture an American motocross title aboard the Swedish-built Husqvarna when he won the 1976 500cc AMA Championship. Howerton followed that championship with several top-notch seasons for Team Suzuki. *Paul Buckley*

"Jammin' Jimmy" Weinert (middle) was one of the most colorful riders on the national motocross circuits from the early to mid-1970s. The New York native was one of the few motocrossers to begin his career in dirt track, and was famous for teasing and goading his competition between motos with his guitar and made-up songs about beating them in the next race. Primarily associated with Kawasaki throughout most of his career, Weinert lays claim to being the first AMA Supercross Champion in 1976. *Joe Bonnello*

From 1974 to 1981, Dick Burleson won eight consecutive AMA National Enduro Championships, a record so extraordinary that it may never be broken. Burleson's total domination of national enduro earned him the nickname "King Richard." In addition to his incredible domestic record, Burleson also won an amazing eight consecutive gold medals in the International Six Days Trials (now called the International Six Days Enduro). Among American off-road racers, Burleson is one of the all-time greats. *Lee Klancher*

The Mags

Reading Material for the Moto-Head

Motocross magazines, more than anything else, have been trendsetters for the sport from the very beginning. They've always been the first place for fans and riders to get a sneak peek at next year's bikes, the coolest new riding gear, and the latest rumors and news from the factory racing world. Along with that, many of the mags feature tips on bike setup and racing techniques to give amateur racers a better chance of winning a trophy on Sunday. One could even argue that the roots of freestyle were actually spawned by magazine test riders back in the 1970s, when they started doing "radical," never-before-seen moves such as "Fender-Kissers" and "One-Footed Tailwhips."

Today there are more motocross mags on the newsstand than ever before, and many of them are at least five times as thick as they were in the early days. Listed here are the most popular and influential motocross mags in America today, along with a quick note on what makes them cool.

Dirt Bike

The original motocross magazine is the oldest in the bunch, dating back to 1971. *Dirt Bike* gets the credit for creating many of the motocross photography techniques still used today.

Cycle News

More a newspaper than a magazine, this weekly has been around for 40 years and is probably the most influential motocross publication in the industry. Because *Cycle News* is published weekly, it's first with all the breaking news, rumors, and race results. Also covers road racing, trials, flat track, etc.

Previous page: One of the most accomplished motojournalists is Jimmy Lewis, who has served as the off-road editor at *Cycle World* magazine and is currently editor-in-chief at *Dirt Rider*. Lewis has competed and finished well in some of the toughest races in the world, including Paris to Dakar, the Endurocross, and Last Man Standing. *Joe Bonnello*

Davey Coombs is the editor of *Racer X* magazine and an announcer for television coverage of Supercross races. *Simon Cudby*

Motocross Action

Started in the 1970s, *MXA* puts much of its effort into bike and product tests and technical how-to articles along with provocative editorials on the current state of the racing world.

Dirt Rider

This mag became a force in the early 1980s and features a well-rounded lineup of bike tests, adventure rides, how-to articles, and riding tips designed to appeal to both racers and trail riders.

Transworld Motocross

A splashy, photo-driven look at motocross racing, with a bit of freestyle material thrown in for good measure. In the early 1990s, this was the first motocross magazine to feature big photo spreads that showed how spectacular the sport really is.

Racer X

The ultimate motocross fan magazine is packed each month with tons of well-written, in-depth articles on racing personalities, events, and motocross history and features some of the best photography in the business. *Racer X* also boasts the largest number of monthly columns written by the racers themselves.

PitRacer

All the features of the other motocross mags except it's all about pitbike racing!

Back in the Day

The History of Motocross

Motocross is usually said to have begun after World War II, but the sport actually originated in cross-country races known as scrambles in England and North America during the 1920s.

The first was the so-called Southern Scott Scramble, held on March 29, 1924, over a 2- to 5-mile cross-country course on Camberley Heath, England. The winner of the 50-mile race was Arthur Sparks, with a time of 2 hours, 1 minute, 51 seconds. In 1926, the Crotona, New York, Motorcycle Club started a similar type of race, but it was called a Tourist Trophy, undoubtedly after the famous Isle of Man road race. It doesn't appear that the Crotona members knew about the scrambles that were becoming so popular among motorcyclists in England. But within a few years, cross-country races were being called scrambles in both the United States and Canada.

Sometime between 1924 and 1934, depending on which account you believe, the scramble crossed the English Channel into France. The French came up with the term "motocross," from "motorcycle" and "cross-country," and developed a new, shorter course with man-made obstacles such as jumps.

One of the first major sports events in Europe after World War II was an international team motocross competition hosted by the Netherlands in 1947. Only two other countries, Belgium and Great Britain, took part. The race comprised two heats of eight laps each over a 2-mile course, with team scores based on the times of the three fastest riders. The British team won by just nine seconds over Belgium. As it turned out, that was the first Motocross des Nations, which has been conducted by the Fédération Internationale de Motocyclisme (FIM) since 1949.

The FIM inaugurated a European individual championship for 500cc-displacement bikes in 1952. That became a world championship event in 1957. The 250cc class was added in 1962.

Scrambles were staged in North America throughout the 1930s and immediately after World War II, but the first race referred to as

In the mid-1970s, factory motocross riders such as Kent Howerton (pictured), Marty Smith, and Bob Hannah became stars with their salaried rides, box vans, and a mechanic or two. They were still a long way from the huge semi-haulers and support teams that can number up to a dozen that the factory riders enjoy today. *Paul Buckley*

motocross was held in Grafton, Vermont, in 1959. The promoter was a dealer for the German-made Maico, then one of the world's best motocross bikes.

But it was a California dealer for Husqvarna of Sweden who really made motocross a popular sport in the United States. Edison Dye was an aeronautical engineer and motorcyclist who began organizing motorcycle tours of Europe during the early 1960s. During one of those tours, Dye saw and fell in love with the Husqvarna. He agreed to become the make's first U.S. distributor and decided that the best way to publicize the bike was to demonstrate it in motocross races.

In the fall of 1966, Dye hired Sweden's Torsten Hallman, the reigning 250cc world champion, to race a Husqvarna in American events. Hallman scored easy victories in several races, including the Canadian Northwest Motocross Championship. But there wasn't enough motocross racing in the United States to get the "Husky" the kind of publicity Dye was looking for, so in 1967 he organized his own series, the Inter-America, better known as the Inter-Am. He brought over several more Europeans to race against Hallman and U.S. scramble riders. The series not only proved popular with existing fans, it created new fans for this kind of motorcycle racing.

At the time, the American Motorcyclist Association wasn't involved in international racing. A very small organization, Motorcycle International Clubs of the United States (MICUS), represented the United States in the FIM. Dye's series was sanctioned by MICUS.

Bob "Hurricane" Hannah celebrates another moto victory during his reign in the late 1970s to early 1980s. *Paul Buckley*

In 1970, the AMA joined the FIM. The association's first major move into international competition was the establishment of the Trans-AMA motocross series to compete against Dye's Inter-Am. The Inter-Am was forced out of business in 1971, but Dye continued promoting races within the Trans-Am series until 1974.

Great Britain had dominated the sport for the first two decades, winning 15 of 20 of the annual Motocross des Nations championships. Then Belgium took over, winning seven championships from 1969 through 1980. In 1981, a young United States team won the Motocross des Nations by just one point over Great Britain. That victory was generally considered a fluke at the time, but it was just the first in a string of 13 consecutive championships for the United States.

Although motocross became very popular in the United States, it didn't fit into the country's standard motorsports format: an oval track with vehicles continually passing a grandstand full of spectators. So Supercross was created.

Supercross is really nothing more than motocross on an artificial course constructed inside a stadium. Surprisingly, it wasn't a uniquely American idea, even though the sport really took off in the United States. Motocross races were run in a stadium outside Paris in August of 1948 and in a Prague, Czechoslovakia, stadium in May of 1956. The Prague event drew an estimated 100,000 fans. There were also some stadium motocross events held in Norway during the 1960s.

Mark "The Bomber" Barnett skies his early 1980s Suzuki over the infield Supercross at the Daytona International Speedway. *Paul Buckley*

Even before motocross was known in the United States, the 1961 Florida State Scramble Championship was staged at Miami Stadium. But Supercross was really rooted in a series of races staged in 1968 by promoter J. C. Agajanian at his Ascot Speedway in Gardena, California. Ironically, the AMA wouldn't sanction the races because they weren't run over "completely natural terrain," as specified in the association's rule book.

That rule had been changed by March of 1971, when a motocross event was promoted by NASCAR founder Bill France in the infield of his Daytona International Speedway. It was successful, so France did it again the following year.

Four months later came the event that gave Supercross its name: The Superbowl of Motocross, staged at the Los Angeles Memorial Coliseum on July 8, 1972, by Mike Goodwin, a rock music promoter. The event drew 28,000 fans, with the second Super-bowl of Motocross drawing 38,000.

Motocross Action magazine referred to the event as the Super-cross. Despite Goodwin's objections, the name stuck. However, the AMA called this version of the sport "stadium motocross" until 1988, when "Supercross" became official.

By then, Supercross had become considerably different from moto-cross. Because of the limited area, which required much tighter courses, it had been different to start with. On the tighter courses, smaller motorcycles were faster than the large machines used on natural motocross courses. In 1976, the AMA made 250cc two-stroke the main class for stadium motocross, as opposed to 500cc for standard motocross.

The most recent revolution in the motocross world has been the switch from bikes powered by two-stroke engines to those powered by four-strokes. For nearly all of motocross history, two-stroke dirt bikes ruled the roost because of their much better power-to-weight ratio and ease of modification and main-tenance. However, during the late 1990s many manufacturers put their efforts into building high-performance four-stroke motocross bikes in anticipation of stricter pollution controls for future off-road vehicles.

Motocross in America really came into its own in the 1980s when bike sales grew, new tracks popped up, and the factories began to support amateur racers as well as the pros with contingency monies. *Paul Buckley*

Of course, in a head-to-head race of motocross bikes with the same cubic-centimeter displacement, a four-stroke wouldn't stand a chance, so the AMA allowed 250cc four-strokes

Unlike the stick and ball sports where fans have little access to the top pros, motocross stars are generally very approachable on race day. Doug Henry has been a fan favorite for well over a decade and has signed hundreds of t-shirts and hats. *Paul Buckley*

to compete in the 125cc two-stroke class and 450cc four-strokes to race in the premier 250cc two-stroke class. At first the four-strokes were only somewhat competitive with the "ringy-dings," but eventually the "thumpers" have come to dominate the sport to the point that there's generally fewer than a handful of two-strokes in any given Supercross or pro motocross championship main event.

There are not too many sports where you can get as close to the action as you can at an outdoor motocross race. Veteran fans know to cover the top of their drinks when the field blasts into the first turn. *Paul Buckley*

Below: Vintage Jeremy McGrath finds him sighting a landing on his factory 1995 Honda CR250. The true roots of motocross can be traced back all the way to events called "scrambles" held in the United States and England back in the 1920s. *Paul Buckley*

A young Ricky Carmichael contemplates what the new millennium will bring to his sport and career. How about the longest winning streak ever recorded? *Paul Buckley*

Crash and Burn!

Crash and Burn!

When Bad Things Happen to Good Racers

Crashing is part of racing. In this section, some of the common (and not-so-common) crashes that occur in motocross racing are shown. We'd tell you not to try this at home, but we are aware that if you decide to race, you will find yourself attempting one of these maneuvers. Note that none of the riders in the photos suffered serious injuries.

A s in any type of motorsports, things can get pretty ugly when riders trip over "the ragged edge." In motocross, crashes tend to be quite spectacular as bikes tumble and riders flail through the air like rag dolls. However, there is a method to this madness as riders and fans over the years have actually given names to the various ways one dismounts from an out-of-control motorcycle. For example, when a rider returns to the pits after a tough moto and reports to his crew that someone "high-sided" and caused him to "endo" over the hay bales, the crew can quickly picture exactly what happened.

The Body Slam (previous spread)
This common crash can be performed off a variety of track obstacles and can even be accomplished on fast, rough straightaways. The key ingredient to a good body slam is that the wind gets knocked out of the rider upon impact. Getting hit by your bike a split second later is optional. *Steve Casper*

The Loopout
This crash is so simple that even beginners can do it well on the first try. Most loopouts occur right off the starting line when a novice rider grabs too much throttle and has his weight too far back. Advanced riders, such as the one pictured here, perform their high-speed loopouts while landing from a jump. *Steve Casper*

From a photographer's point of view, capturing a motocross wreck with a camera is not an easy thing to do. In the first place, the photographer has to be lucky enough to be at the right place at the right time during the race. Second, things happen so quickly during an accident that focus, framing, and timing are critical to capturing the peak moment of impact.

Since motocross crashes have been around since the very beginning of the sport,

let's take this opportunity to travel back in time and look at some classic wrecks from the past. Keep in mind that nearly all of the riders pictured here walked away from their wipeouts and were back at the track the next week. Safety gear such as helmets, boots, goggles, gloves, and chest protectors have helped save a lot of skin over the years and are a must for racers and trail riders alike.

The Me-Too Syndrome

If the guy next to you is grabbing all the attention with a major wahoo, then you'd better perform a quick Flying W to get the spotlight back on yourself. In 1989 at the Kansas City amateur Supercross race this particular type of wreck took out half of the 250cc class on the first lap. *Steve Casper*

The Train Wreck

Nearly everyone who races motocross has had to endure the pain and embarrassment of falling in the middle of the first turn on a start at least once. The train wreck can quickly spawn a variety of offshoot crashes such as the T-bone, knobbie nose, and the especially gruesome sprocket kanuckler. *Steve Casper*

The "I Hear Many Bikes, Kemosabe" Crash

This position actually offers a few side benefits such as listening for pinging in the exhaust, checking knobby sidebite traction with your cheek, and making sure your footpegs are lubed and folding when the bike slams into your hip. *Steve Casper*

The Lowside

This is probably the very first crash most dirt bikers experience. Simply go into a corner a little too fast, lose the front end, and fall to the "low" side. The humiliating face plant typically follows this relatively harmless spill. *Steve Casper*

The Endo

This frightening crash begins when a rider lands front-wheel down off a jump and is launched into the air before slamming into the ground with his faithful machine right there ready to inflict even further damage. This crash is actually worthwhile if there is a crowd of at least a dozen people there to witness it. Sadly, that was not the case for this amateur Supercross racer. *Steve Casper*

Must-See Races

Classic Events at Spectacular Venues

I t's one thing to see a great handlebar-to-handlebar motocross battle, but when you get to enjoy it at one of the classic events or tracks in the world it's even twice as good. Like the hardcore car-racing fans that congregate annually at the Indy 500 and the Daytona 500, motocross fans look forward to attending their special events year after year. Whether it's the history of the track, the background scenery, the challenge of terrain, or simply the spectacle of the event, certain races stand out as must-see events for many avid fans.

We whittled our list of big events down to what we feel are the 10 must-see motocross races and present them here along with some cool racing shots to help you imagine what it might be like to pass through the ticket gate. Enjoy, and if you ever have the chance to make it to one of these events, go for it!

Motocross des Nations (Previous spread)

This one-of-a-kind event dates back to the 1940s and pits three-man teams of riders from each country against each other to determine which nation reigns supreme. Taking place at a different locale every year, the event was dominated by European riders until the early 1980s, when America became the team to beat. *Simon Cudby*

Hangtown

Nearly every great of American motocross has lined up at the gate of this legendary track in northern California. Back in the 1970s it was known for developing ruts so deep that riders nearly disappeared in them when they fell. *Simon Cudby*

Mammoth (left)

Many would argue that this once-a-year track is the most scenic motocross course in the world. It's built on the same hillside that is used for world-class snow skiing in the winter and draws thousands of amateur and pro riders to its challenging terrain. *Simon Cudby*

Glen Helen

This gritty-looking desert track is the youngest in the group, but has risen to importance by hosting the opening round of the national outdoor circuit every year. Add to that the fastest downhill section in the country and thousands of Southern California spectators jamming themselves onto the hillsides, and you have yourself one classic MX event. *Joe Bonnello*

Bercy Supercross

Supercross is not nearly as big a deal in Europe as it is in the United States, but you would never know that by attending the annual Bercy SX held outside Paris. In a unique way that only the Euros seem capable of doing, the prerace pageantry is mind blowing and usually sets the stage for some pretty good racing. *Joe Bonnello*

Millville

North central fans get a chance to see the stars of motocross compete on a demanding and scenic southern Minnesota track near the Mississippi River. Every year a strange dude dressed as the "Whoop Monster" rides around in a souped-up golf cart greeting (and scaring!) the spectators. *Simon Cudby*

Red Bud

This midwestern gem is located in the southwest corner of Michigan and features spectacular jumps, uphills, and downhills set within park-like woods and rolling grassy knolls. *Joe Bonnello*

Clockwise, from above
Southwick
This Massachusetts MX mainstay is one of the most tiring tracks on the circuit because the sandy course quickly develops monster whoops everywhere. The high-banked, sandy "Daytona" turns also make for some awesome roost photos. *Simon Cudby*

Steel City
Pennsylvania has long been a hotbed of MX action, and the Steel City National is its premiere event. Many championship battles have been settled at Steel City as the race usually falls near the end of the AMA Motocross Championship series. *Simon Cudby*

Winter X Games
Some of the most incredible motocross photography has come out of the Winter X Games as the freestylers flip it and whip it on the snow ramps with incredible mountain scenery as a backdrop. The best part of this event are the free tickets. *Simon Cudby*

149

Ride the World

Ride the World

Ten Off-Road Adventure Rides
To Do Before You Die —by Lee Klancher

When it comes to off-road riding, the world is your oyster. If the local riding is getting a bit long in the tooth, save your pennies and plan a ride with saltwater crocs, Bolivian dignitaries, and Mormon madmen. I won't pretend that this list is complete or authoritative—there are too many amazing places to truly pick out the best— but these are 10 great rides that you shouldn't miss before you get old and decrepit.

Five Miles of Hell
San Rafael Mountains, Utah
Southern Utah is a mecca for off-road riders, whether you're talking about the freestyle adrenaline junkies jumping canyons or the hard-core off-roaders tackling some of America's toughest terrain. Five Miles of Hell is a stretch of trail filled with wicked climbs up rock formations. The trail is at times marked only with a stripe of white paint leading up treacherous climbs that only the most experienced riders should attempt.

Trail Info
Utah Division of Parks and Recreation
1594 West North Temple
Suite 116, Box 146001
Salt Lake City, UT 84114-6001
(801) 538-7220
www.stateparks.utah.gov/ohv/default.htm

Trail Location and Description
www.utahmountainbiking.com/trails/five-hell.htm

Previous spread: Five Miles of Hell is a nasty stretch of trail in the San Rafael Mountains near Green River, Utah. Really more like 7 miles of hell, 2 miles of purgatory, and 11 miles of limbo, the trail crosses shear rock faces and huge drop-offs; it should be attempted only by experienced riders. *Lee Klancher*

The surface of the trail is Coconino sandstone, which is smoother in texture than Moab's slickrock, but has more waves and ripples. *Lee Klancher*

Go past this sign at your own risk. Bring lots of water and plan a full day to cover the 20.1-mile loop. *Lee Klancher*

Bad Roads, Giant Glaciers, and Snow-Capped Ranges
McCarthy, Alaska

If there is a dual-sport heaven, it may be McCarthy, Alaska. Nestled deep in the Wrangell–St. Elias mountain range, this funky little backpacker town is accessible only by a 60-mile stretch of bad gravel road that keeps the casual tourists out. Plenty of off-shoot trails worthy of exploration pepper the road, and you'll find grizzly bears, moose, and snow-capped mountain valleys on the way. Four-wheeled tourists have to hoof it over a narrow bridge into town, but motorcyclists can ride across the bridge and up to the Kennecott mine. The town features good, cheap eats at One Potato and good beers on tap at The New Golden Saloon, a historic tavern in town. Add in trails leading up to the mine and a view of the stunning Kennicott Glacier, and you have a recipe for a motorcycle adventure that's a must-have on any adventure motorcyclist's list.

Trail Info

Wrangell–St. Elias National Park
106.8 Richardson Hwy.
PO Box 439
Copper Center, AK 99573-0439
(907) 822-5234
www.nps.gov/wrst/

Area Info

www.mccarthy-kennicott.com

The Copper River Valley (shown here) is about a six-hour drive from Anchorage. From this point, about 60 miles of rough gravel road lead to the former mining town of McCarthy, Alaska. *Lee Klancher*

The Kennecott Mine was one of the most productive copper mines in the world in the mid-1930s, and employed 600 people at its peak. *Lee Klancher*

McCarthy is nestled in the Wrangell–St. Elias mountain range, one of the largest and most pristine stretches of national park land in America. *Lee Klancher*

Caravana
Bolivia

Once a year, about 100 South Americans and a handful of riders from around the world take their place in Caravana, a nine-day ATV and motorcycle off-road ride in Bolivia that is an annual national celebration. The support crew for the ride is amazing, with another 100 people, dozens of trucks, and several multi-engine aircraft following along. The route is different each year, and the evening activities match the day's hard-core riding in terms of energy and adventure. Each town that the ride visits puts on a festival to celebrate the riders' arrival, with bands playing, food provided, and hundreds of locals lining the streets to offer a rock-star welcome to the Caravana riders. Bolivian television covers the event on the news each night, and the South Americans on the ride include dignitaries from South American governments and some of Bolivia's best riders. The Bolivian beer company Paceña creates a commemorative beer can with the Caravana logo on it, and the riding challenges range from cliff-clinging mountain rides near La Paz to running through the virgin Amazon jungle in the north. An event that's been featured in *Forbes* magazine, as well as most of the enthusiast magazines, this ride can best be described as Mardi Gras plus motorsports madness.

Caravana Contact Info
(591) 3 334-7145
www.caravan-atv.com

If seeing the wilds of Bolivia is your idea of adventure, a tour known as the Caravana delivers with a large group of participants and some of the most remote backcountry on the planet. *Lee Klancher*

Caravana is a national event, and the logo painted on everything from the airplanes th provide support, to T-shirts, and even to a commemorative Paceña beer can. *Lee Klanc*

Singletrack Heaven
Akeley, Minnesota

Northern Minnesota has a small, dedicated off-road scene, and the trail system in the Paul Bunyan State Forest near Akeley, Minnesota, has some of the country's finest singletrack. If you are a fan of flow singletrack—the kind of riding where the challenges are perfect and allow you to reach a Zen-like state, don't miss this system. One of the resident riders, Dan Hanna, likes to say this trail system lets him become "one with the pine needles." Whether or not you reach that riding nirvana, the pine forests, starry nights, and sweet singletrack are worthy of a visit.

Trail Info
Minnesota Department of Natural Resources
(651) 296-6157
www.dnr.state.mn.us/ohv/index.html

Camping and dirt biking go hand-in-hand, and there are plenty of good spots near Akeley, Minnesota. *Lee Klancher*

Above: The terrain near Akeley has enough elevation change to keep things interesting. *Lee Klancher*

Left: If your riding tastes lean toward wicked singletrack, northern Minnesota's trail system in Paul Bunyan State Forest should be added to your list. *Lee Klancher*

Hatfield-McCoy's Hand-Built Singletrack
Manley, West Virginia

You may have heard about the great riding opportunities available for ATV enthusiasts in the Hatfield-McCoy system, but two-wheeled fans shouldn't shy away from this seminal destination. The area features more than 500 miles of dedicated off-road trail that is worth a visit, and the undiscovered gem at HM is the singletrack. Hatfield-McCoy was built by a motorcycle enthusiast who walked the steep rocky terrain of the riding system with a handful of flags and picked out nearly impassable coutes.

He then hired a small crew of guys and told them to build singletrack. "I gave 'em a clapped-out XR250 and told them to keep working until the best rider in the group could barely ride the trail." These stretches of singletrack are not terribly long, but they are well worth the trip, with challenging sidehill routes snaking along the West Virginia mountains. Add in the fact that West Virginians are colorful, friendly folk who don't seem to mind the fact that you can legally ride your dirt bike down Main Street to the trail, and you have a ride worthy of your list.

Trail Info
Hatfield-McCoy Trails
P.O. Box 539
Lyburn, WV 25632
(800) 592-2217
www.trailsheaven.com

The Hatfield-McCoy trail system in West Virginia has more than 500 miles of trails open to OHV use. The gems for motorcycle riders in the system are several custom-built sections of singletrack. *Lee Klancher*

Within the 500 miles of the Hatfield-McCoy trail system are some great dual-sport sections, as well. *Lee Klancher*

The Ozarks
Cass, Arkansas

The Ozarks could be nirvana for the well-rounded motorcyclist. The area offers several dedicated off-road systems, enough for a week of good riding featuring rocky stream crossings, sandy whooped-out forest trails, and singletrack snaking over the mountains. There's also a state full of twisty back roads for the street guy, and the Ozarks are heaven for dual-sporters. Trails cut across the area, some going so far back even the locals aren't sure where they end. If you are lucky enough to dual-sport the Ozarks, bring a big tank and a GPS system—you can get lost in places from which you may never return.

Trail Info

Ozark–St. Francis National Forests
605 West Main
Russellville, AR 72801
(479) 968-2354
www.fs.fed.us/oonf/ozark/index1.html

Ride the Beach
Bahía de Samaná, Dominican Republic

Ever dream of riding beach for 50 miles, crossing waist-deep streams that require you to carry your motorcycle, and ending up staying at a five-star hotel on the beach where they welcome off-road dirt bags? Dream on,

The Ozark Mountains offer several OHV riding parks that offer great singletrack, abundant stream crossings, and challenging, rocky terrain. *Lee Klancher*

because you'll find that and more in the Dominican Republic. The country has a dedicated off-road racing scene, and some of those racers serve as tour guides on this ride that departs from Santa Domingo and threads its way north to the aforementioned beach bonanza. And if you want good hardcore riding rather than the watered-down dual-sporting offered by too many adventure tour companies, this group will deliver. The country is littered with a mix of narrow, brutal dirt roads and true singletrack, and the tour guides are hard-core riders who know the best routes in the country.

Trail Info
Coastal MotoAdventures
(809) 885-2772
www.coastalmotoadventures.com

The Dominican Republic offers some of the best riding in the world. *Lee Klancher*

A ferry ride crosses the Bahía de Samaná on the north side of the Dominican Republic. *Lee Klancher*

Mike's Sky Ranch
Baja California, Mexico

If you haven't heard of Mike's, well, where the hell have you been? This sleepy resort in the San Rafael mountains of Baja is one of the essential off-road destinations in North America. The riding opportunities are endless, with a myriad of trails leading into the mountain range surrounding the ranch. Parts of the Baja 1000 race course run nearby, and the rock-and-sand-strewn trails are rugged, challenging, and fast. The rooms at Mike's are well suited to housing off-road riders, meaning that your significant other would probably be a bit put off by the beat-up mattresses and, umm, earthy finish of the rooms, but the price is right ($25 and up), and the bar downstairs makes up for it with homemade flour tortillas, fire-roasted *carnitas*, and plenty of cold Dos Equis. Add the bar walls covered with 50 years' worth of posters, cards, and notes pinned up by off-roaders and you have a destination that's rich in Baja lore and history to go with the terrific riding.

Trail Info
Mike's Sky Ranch
www.mikesskyranch.com
011-52-664-68-15514

The Baja coast is only a few hours ride from Mike's Sky Ranch. *Lee Klancher*

Baja, California, is a paradise for off-road riders. *Lee Klancher*

161

Castillo Ranch
Central California

The privately owned track at Castillo Ranch features a layout designed to take advantage of the naturally hilly terrain of the area. The result is short on steep doubles and long on fun. A built-in watering system keeps the surface perfectly prepped, and the track features plenty of stomach-churning elevation changes. The result is one of the most entertaining motocross tracks in the country.

The Telegraph Track
Cape York, Australia

Northeastern Australia is an enchanting mix of rain-forested mountains, pristine beaches, the Great Barrier Reef, and a several-hundred-mile-long stretch of bad road known as the Telegraph Track leading to Cape York, at the northernmost tip of the country. The road is littered with stream crossings that require snorkel systems on the off-road trucks that make the trip, and will challenge the skills of

The Castillo Ranch in Southern California is a motocross lover's dream. *Simon Cudby*

off-road motorcyclists. The reward at the end of this grueling journey is a stunning view off the towering rock on the north side of the country, Pajinka. Don't be fooled by the allure of the blue-green tropical waters off the deserted beaches up there—heavy populations of great white sharks, poisonous jellyfish, and saltwater crocodiles make swimming risky business in Cape York. That's the price you pay for riding to one of the world's most beautiful remote places.

Trail Info
Stay Upright Motorcycle Tours
www.stayupright.com.au/offroad_tours.htm
61 (02) 8824 9980

The northeastern corner of Australia is known as Cape York. This is the northernmost tip of Australia's mainland, a rock called Pajinka. Thursday Island is visible in the distance, with Papua New Guinea just over 100 miles off the coast. A rugged road, the Telegraph Trail, is the only way to drive to this remote part of the world. *Lee Klancher*

The Telegraph Track is filled with stream crossings and crosses rainforest and barren outback. *Lee Klancher*

Cape York is legendary for its population of salt water crocodiles, which grow to more than 20 feet. *Lee Klancher*

Joe Bonnello

Dirty Films

The Best Motocross Movies and Videos

Over the years, Hollywood has tried to capture the excitement of dirt bike racing on the big screen. Some, like 1971's *On Any Sunday,* changed the lives of many of the young people who saw it by drawing them into the sport. Others, like *Supercross: The Movie* (2005), sent thousands of motocross fans out of theaters shaking their heads and wondering if they'd ever seen a worse movie in their life!

With the advent of affordable video production equipment in the 1990s, virtually anyone with a few thousand bucks could make their own "film," and a whole new breed of motorcycle entertainment was created.

The following is a list of what we think are the 5 best dirt bike and motocross films and DVDs of all time, along with some bonus categories. So the next time you're looking for something to do on a Friday night, grab one of these classics and try not to get any dirt in your popcorn!

Top 5 Dirt Bike Films/Videos of All Time

On Any Sunday (1971): This documentary film about all forms of dirt biking inspired thousands of young people to take up the relatively new sport in the early 1970s. The scene of Steve McQueen and Malcolm Smith doing donuts on the beach is considered to be nirvana by many dirt bikers.

Crusty Demons of Dirt I (1994): This is the video that basically started the whole motocross freestyle craze. Anyone who watches it will never forget Seth Enslow's ill-fated dune launch into the stratosphere.

Dust to Glory (2005): Filmed by Dana Brown, the son of Don Brown (who did *On Any Sunday*), this documentary captures the magic of the Baja 1000. Although there's a fair amount of car and truck stuff as well, dirt bikers seem to love this DVD.

Terrafirma 1 (1994): A groundbreaking extreme video that came out the same year as *Crusty Demons.* This one features interviews with Ricky Carmichael, Bubba Stewart, and

Travis Pastrana from their mini days. Like *Crusty Demons*, many sequels of the same name follow *Terrafirma*.

Little Fauss and Big Halsy (1970): Robert Redford starred in this feature-length movie about two motocross racers traveling the circuit. One reviewer said, "I'm certain those predisposed to cornpone comedy and rustic sentimentality find it very nearly a work of art."

Best Motocross Videos for Kids

Motocrossed (2001): Made by the Disney Channel, this fun film tells the story of a girl motocross racer who disguises herself as her brother and starts beating the boys.

Motocross Kids (2004): When the star rider gets injured (oh, now there's something we've never seen before!), the crew enlists a chimp to run in the big race (well, that's a new one!).

Michael, Michael Motorcycle (2003): This short (30 minute) DVD is aimed at the really little kids and by all accounts they love it! It's even educational and stresses safety first. From a dad who reviewed it: "It sure beats the heck out of that purple dinosaur!"

Worst Motocross Movie of All Time

Supercross: The Movie [also released as *Supercross*] (2005): Folks in the motorcycle industry were expecting the best from this ambitious Hollywood offering but ended up getting a motocross version of *Plan 9 from Outer Space*. The plot, characters, and acting couldn't be any lamer and the racing footage is just plain weird. Sample line: "My name's Trip Carlyle. This is my brother, K.C. We're tight, but that doesn't mean we don't compete."

Best Dirt Bike Scene in Any Movie

The Great Escape (1963): What could possibly be better than World War II prisoner of war Steve McQueen fleeing the Nazis on a motorcycle and jumping over a border fence to freedom in Switzerland? The film is based on a true story to boot. Racer Bud Ekins performed the actual jump on a stock '62 Triumph street bike. He flew 12 feet high and sailed 65 feet into an *uphill landing* on a 400-pound bike with only a couple inches of suspension travel. "It just went bang and then it bounced," Ekins recalls today. "We got it done first take."

Most Illogical Plot in a Motocross Movie

Winners Take All (1987): Near the end of the movie, our hero's bike is stolen even though he just qualified for the big race the next day. His racing buddies who didn't make the race pitch in and feverishly build him a new bike from the ground up with spare parts. The funny part is, didn't all those guys have race bikes all ready to go sitting in the back of their pickups since they didn't qualify for the big race?

Honorable Mentions

The Wild One (1953): This *proto*-biker flick set the stage for all that followed and has harmed the image of motorcyclists so much that its influence still lingers. However, the opening seen where Johnny (Marlon Brando) and his gang gate crash a scrambles event and do a few laps on their street bikes in the middle of the race is great cinema in our book.

Easy Rider (1969): Sure, it's all street stuff, but the "rebel biker" attitude found in this groundbreaking movie is classic.

Moto-Speak

Talk the Talk

Motocross riders and fans sometimes seem like they have a language all their own. The following are some terms and expressions you may hear at the track.

Basket case: An old bike that probably doesn't run. Often many engine and transmission parts have been removed and are either missing or stored in the trunk or a "basket."

Block pass: When one rider passes and aggressively cuts in front of another. In some cases, physical contact is made.

Blue groove: When the dirt on the track is very dry and hard packed and it appears blue or black from the rubber worn off of tires.

Bottomed out: When a bike's shocks are completely compressed due to a hard landing.

Came in hot: When a rider carries a lot of momentum into a corner.

Came up short: When a rider fails to completely clear an obstacle.

Cased it: When a rider misjudges the distance of a jump and the bottom of the bike hits the ground.

Dead sailor: When a rider jumps over a freestyle jump and doesn't attempt a trick.

Face plant: When a rider crashes and lands on his face.

Goon: An outdated, inappropriate, dangerous, or squirrelly rider. Also: Spode, Nerd, Dork, Squirrel.

Panic rev: The typical reaction when a frightened rider sees that his front end is low in the air. The rider can sometimes bring the front end up by hitting the throttle.

Pinned: A bike that's at its maximum RPM.

Stoppie: When a rider pulls in the front brake causing the bike to pitch forward into an endo-wheelie and continues moving.

Stuffed: When one rider passes another on a corner and forces him to the outside edge of the track.

Swap: When the back end of a bike jumps to the right and left, usually caused by bumps in the course.

Tapped out: The top speed of each gear on a bike. For example, "I was tapped out in third."

T-Bone: When one rider runs directly into the side of another rider and usually takes them out.

Washed out: Any time a rider's front tire slides out to one side or the other.

Mini Mania

Where the Stars of Tomorrow Hone Their Skills

It seems that just about any bio you read about the top pro motocross racers begins by mentioning that they got started racing minicycles, usually at a very young age like five or six! It only makes sense that the more track time you have under your belt by the time you reach your teens, the faster you're going to be.

Racing motocross on a regular basis year after year requires substantial dedication and discipline from both the child and his family, but nearly all of them will agree that the rewards are well worth the sacrifices. Sure, only a handful of the thousands of minicycle racers in the country will ever make a living in the sport of motocross, but each one will be able to fondly look back at all those Sundays with family as some of the most exciting times of their lives.

The biggest and most prestigious event for minicycle and amateur teen racers in the United States is the annual pilgrimage to Loretta Lynn's Dude Ranch in central Tennessee every summer for the AMA Amateur National Championships. Over a five-day period, full gates of riders (who had to qualify for the nationals in a series of qualifiers that were held throughout the country) compete in three brutal motos over the challenging course in the heat and humidity of August. Virtually all of the top American-bred riders today, including Ricky Carmichael and James Stewart, have won numerous minicycle titles at Loretta Lynn's. In fact, many of the factory teams send representatives to Loretta Lynn's to scout for the next big talents in motocross.

Previous spread: There is lot more to motocross racing than just the action on the track, and many of the top riders today learned that at an early age when they hauled their machines around trying to ride as many events as possible. Of course, most mini riders never turn pro, but the memories of quality time spent with their families at the racetrack last a lifetime. *Simon Cudby*

Minicycle racing is bigger than ever than these days, with more machines and events to choose from, although it appears that the hot setup in this class is to have a yellow brand of bike! In full-field situations like this, young riders quickly learn the importance of getting the holeshot. *Simon Cudby*

Simon Cudby

You'll find a lot more girls racing in the mini classes than in the bigger-motored divisions. Why that is, we can only speculate, but these two riders at the Loretta Lynn's Amateur Nationals sure seem to be enjoying themselves. *Simon Cudby*

Old-time motocrossers just shake their heads when they see what some of the kids these days are capable of jumping with their little, high-strung motorcycles. In fact, for two-stroke aficionados, minis are about the only class they can practice their hop-up and wrenching skills on. *Simon Cudby*

Now c'mon, we all know that the little guys are only interested in racing, right? *Simon Cudby*

While most of their pals are spending their Sundays at the soccer field or baseball lot, these kids are revving their engines on the starting line in anticipation of a high-flying, hang-on-tight thrill ride that's like no other in the world of sports. *Simon Cudby*

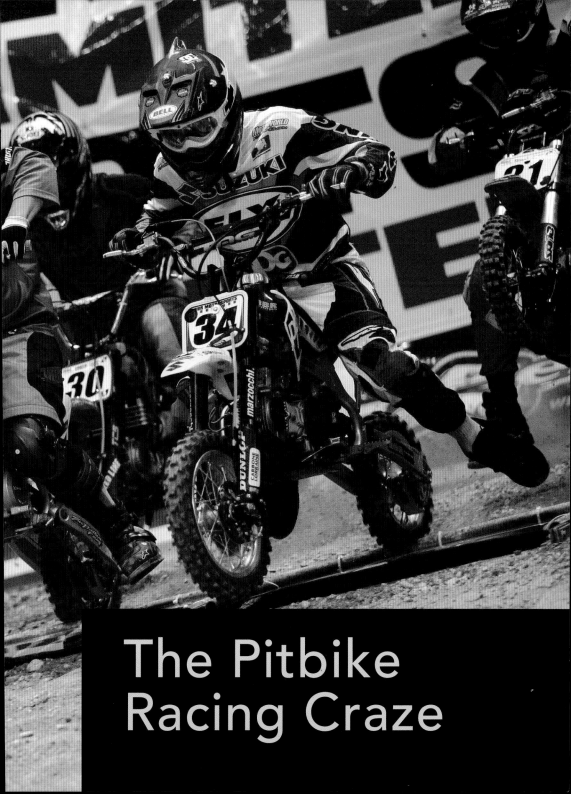

The Pitbike
Racing Craze

Backyard Racing Turns Pro

Pitbike (noun) pit' bik (plural: pitbikes) 1) a small-motored minibike that pit-dads, pitmoms, and pitmechanics use to putt around in the pits; 2) a hopped-up, small-motored minibike that adult riders use to race motocross, either in the backyard or on full-sized motocross tracks. (*See also* "pitbike babes," "pitbike nationals," and "how to lose a fortune chasing your adolescent fantasies.")

As you can see, Webster's had to make a few changes to their original definition of pitbike. Legend has it that the craze started back in the late 1980s when a suburban Southern California family man named Bobby Langlin built a BMX track in the tiny confines of his fenced-in backyard. Being a motocross enthusiast as well, Langlin one day took a few laps on a mild-mannered, four-stroke pitbike and found that it was a hoot. When he invited a few pals over with their pitbikes for a little play racing, the sport was born. It gained national attention when magazines started covering his Langtown Backyard Nationals that eventually offered a pro purse and attracted more spectators than his backyard could handle. Langtown only happens once a year—Langlin still has next-door neighbors after all!

Today pitbike, or mini moto, racing is a legitimate branch of motocross with several big series held throughout the country, including the $15,000 Mini Moto Supercross that takes place annually in the Orleans Arena in Las Vegas. Pitbike racing enthusiasts even have their own monthly magazines.

Unlike regular motocross, where one can buy a machine capable of winning right off the showroom floor, stock pitbikes need a ton of modifications to win on the track. The hop-up shops have willingly obliged racers by offering super-modified racers ready to go, but at considerable cost. No one seems to mind because the sport is booming. And when you think about it, what could be more fun than being a kid again!

Previous spread: Big guys on small bikes. Sounds like a joke, but it's serious business for these guys, who are racing at a big-dollar pitbike race in Las Vegas. *Simon Cudby*

Handlebars and footpegs need to be custom fitted for most of the riders in the pitbike class. Of course, the smaller and lighter adults do have an advantage. *Simon Cudby*

Pitbike racers don't skimp on the riding gear. In fact, contact between riders is quite common since the speed of these machines isn't quite up to par with the bigger classes.
Simon Cudby

184

Dozens of motorcycle hop-up shops specialize in pitbike racers, many of which dump more dough into their machines than the full-size bike racers do, since so many mods are required to be competitive at the top levels in this type of racing. *Simon Cudby*

Women Behind Bars

Women Turn Pro

Women's riding expertise and fierce competitive spirit date back 60 years to the 1940s, when daring women raced Velocettes, BSAs, and Matchless 500s across the then-vast wilderness. As the feminist movement took shape in the 1960s, women also made their way in the sports arena and on the racetrack.

Since women's motocross was first organized on a national level in the late 1960s, there have been many twists and turns with the various sanctioning bodies. Today the Women's Motocross Association (WMA) runs a national series of events for pro women racers and also offers amateur and youth classes.

Previous spread: The Women's Motocross Assocation (WMA) hosts events around the country and a national championship. Top racers attract industry sponsorship and magazine coverage. Jessica Patterson's Honda CRF250 wore the number one plate for the 2006 season. *Joe Bonnello*

Right: Sarah Whitmore has been winning women's motocross titles since 1998, and she is one of the top WMA riders on the circuit. A native of Cheybogan, Michigan, she rides a Yamaha YZ250F. *Joe Bonnello*

Left: The WMA has a charter with the American Motorcyclist Assocation, and was founded when the Women's Motocross League dissolved in 2004. Kirsten Raemisch of Madison, Wisconsin, races the No. 19 YZ250F. *Joe Bonnello*

Joe Bonnello

Joe Bonnello

INDEX

彼 得 兔 和 他 的 朋 友 们

点点鼠夫人的故事

[英] 毕翠克丝·波特/著　孙静/译

西南师范大学出版社

图书在版编目（CIP）数据

点点鼠夫人的故事 / （英）毕翠克丝·波特著；孙静译. -- 重庆：西南师范大学出版社，2016.8
（彼得兔和他的朋友们）
ISBN 978-7-5621-8083-8

Ⅰ. ①点… Ⅱ. ①毕… ②孙… Ⅲ. ①儿童文学—图画故事—英国—现代 Ⅳ. ①I561.85

中国版本图书馆 CIP 数据核字（2016）第 163964 号

点点鼠夫人的故事　　　　　　　　　[英]毕翠克丝·波特/著　　孙静/译
diandianshu furen de gushi

责任编辑： 胡秀英
装帧设计： 甘　霖
出版发行： 西南师范大学出版社
　　　　　　　地址：重庆市北碚区天生路 2 号
　　　　　　　邮编：400715
　　　　　　　网址：www.xscbs.com
经　销： 全国新华书店
印　刷： 湖北楚天传媒印务有限责任公司
开　本： 710 mm×1000mm　　　1/16
印　张： 2.75
字　数： 22 千字
版　次： 2016 年 8 月第 1 版
印　次： 2017 年 3 月第 2 次印刷
书　号： ISBN 978-7-5621-8083-8

定　价： 12.00 元

☆☆☆

序　言

　　"彼得兔"系列故事的作者是英国女性作家暨插画家毕翠克丝·波特（Helen Beatrix Potter）。故事诞生于波特写给她家庭教师五岁儿子的信。这位家庭老师的儿子卧病在床，波特为了安慰他，在信中讲了这个故事，并且在故事当中鼓励他。

　　波特姐弟小的时候收养了许多小动物，有兔子、蜥蜴、青蛙、蛇、睡鼠、狗、刺猬等，每个动物都有一个名字。波特以她特有的绘画天赋和对艺术的敏感，用好玩的故事和生动可爱的图画记录了动物们在成长中发生的故事，这些小动物后来就成了"彼得兔"系列故事中的各种角色，并最终成就了"彼得兔"系列故事的辉煌。

　　本丛书内容从孩子的角度出发，文字流畅清新且富于童趣，读起来朗朗上口，有助于培养孩子对故事阅读的兴趣，以及增强孩子对故事的理解和记忆能力，让孩子在故事中享受童年的快乐！

CONTENTS

目 录

点点鼠夫人的故事

<ruby>从<rt>cóng</rt></ruby><ruby>前<rt>qián</rt></ruby>，<ruby>有<rt>yǒu</rt></ruby><ruby>一<rt>yì</rt></ruby><ruby>只<rt>zhī</rt></ruby><ruby>丛<rt>cóng</rt></ruby><ruby>林<rt>lín</rt></ruby><ruby>鼠<rt>shǔ</rt></ruby>，<ruby>人<rt>rén</rt></ruby><ruby>们<rt>men</rt></ruby><ruby>都<rt>dōu</rt></ruby><ruby>叫<rt>jiào</rt></ruby><ruby>她<rt>tā</rt></ruby><ruby>点<rt>diǎn</rt></ruby><ruby>点<rt>diǎn</rt></ruby><ruby>鼠<rt>shǔ</rt></ruby><ruby>夫<rt>fū</rt></ruby><ruby>人<rt>rén</rt></ruby>。<ruby>她<rt>tā</rt></ruby><ruby>住<rt>zhù</rt></ruby><ruby>在<rt>zài</rt></ruby><ruby>树<rt>shù</rt></ruby><ruby>篱<rt>lí</rt></ruby><ruby>边<rt>biān</rt></ruby><ruby>上<rt>shang</rt></ruby><ruby>的<rt>de</rt></ruby><ruby>一<rt>yí</rt></ruby><ruby>个<rt>gè</rt></ruby><ruby>沙<rt>shā</rt></ruby><ruby>洞<rt>dòng</rt></ruby><ruby>里<rt>li</rt></ruby>。

zhè shì yí tào hěn yǒu
这是一套很有

qù de fáng zi fáng zi li
趣的房子！房子里

yǒu yì tiáo tiáo jiāo cuò de shā
有一条条交错的沙

tǔ zǒu dào fēn bié tōng wǎng
土走道，分别通往

chǔ cáng shì jiān guǒ shōu cáng shì zhǒng zi shōu cáng shì tā men quán dōu shì
储藏室、坚果收藏室、种子收藏室……它们全都是

shùn zhe shù gēn xiū jiàn de
顺着树根修建的。

当然，这里也少不了厨房、客厅、卧室、餐具室
和食品室。点点鼠夫人的床其实是用一个小箱子
做成的！她每天就在这张床上睡觉。

diǎn diǎn shǔ fū rén shì yì
点点鼠夫人是一

zhī yǒu jié pǐ de xiǎo lǎo shǔ
只有洁癖的小老鼠。

tā zǒng shì zài qīng lǐ dǎ sǎo
她总是在清理、打扫

tā nà róu ruǎn de shā dì bǎn
她那柔软的沙地板。

yǒu shí hou tā yào shi zài gān jìng de shā tǔ zǒu dào shang yù dào yì zhī mí
有时候，她要是在干净的沙土走道上遇到一只迷

lù de jiǎ chóng jiù huì qiāo zhe tā de bò ji dà shēng shuō qù qù
路的甲虫，就会敲着她的簸箕大声说："去！去！

xiǎo zāng jiǎo
小脏脚！"

4

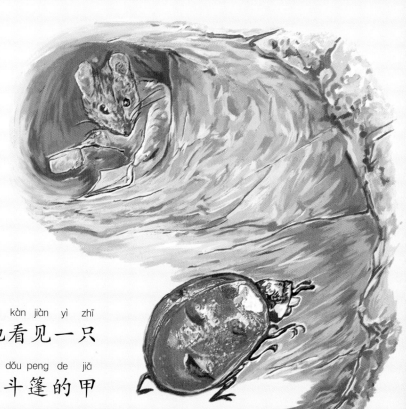

有一天，她看见一只
身穿红色斑点斗篷的甲
虫在她的洞口来回打转，
立即喊道："瓢虫妈妈，您的房子着火了！
快飞回去救您的孩子们吧！"

5

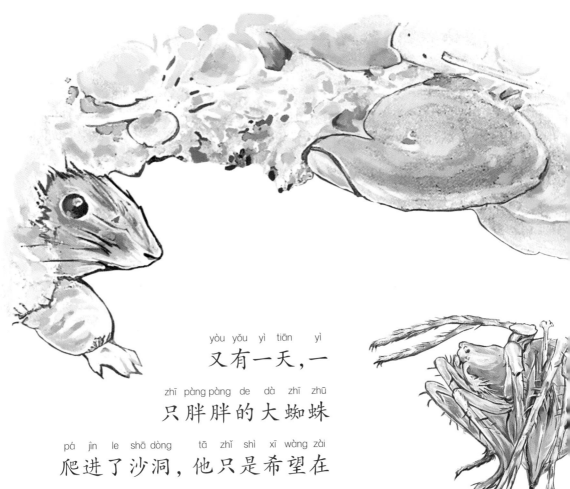

又有一天，一只胖胖的大蜘蛛爬进了沙洞，他只是希望在这里避避雨。点点鼠夫人恼怒地对蜘蛛大叫："走开，你这大胆的坏家伙！竟敢把蜘蛛网挂在我这干净的屋子里！"

她立即把蜘蛛赶了出去。那只蜘蛛赶忙攀着一根长长的细丝爬了出去。

一天，点点鼠夫人想去储藏室拿樱桃核和蓟花种子来当晚餐。她在走道里边走边闻来闻去，还仔细地盯着地板："有蜜蜂进来过！我确信，我可以辨认出那些小脏脚印。"

突然，在一个拐角，她遇到了一只大黄蜂。点点鼠夫人严肃地看着大黄蜂，她真希望自己手中有把扫帚！"你好，大黄蜂。你到这里来干什么？为什么你总是从窗口飞进我的家来？"点点鼠夫人有些生气了。

"嗡嗡嗡！"大黄蜂也
wēng wēng wēng   dà huáng fēng yě

生气地叫道。点点鼠夫人不想再理她，便走向一
shēng qì de jiào dào   diǎn diǎn shǔ fū rén bù xiǎng zài lǐ tā   biàn zǒu xiàng yì

间储存橡子的储藏室。橡子早就吃完了，所以这
jiān chǔ cún xiàng zi de chǔ cáng shì   xiàng zi zǎo jiù chī wán le   suǒ yǐ zhè

间储藏室应该是空的；可是，点点鼠夫人却发现里
jiān chǔ cáng shì yīng gāi shì kōng de   kě shì   diǎn diǎn shǔ fū rén què fā xiàn lǐ

面堆满了乱七八糟的干苔藓。
miàn duī mǎn le luàn qī bā zāo de gān tái xiǎn

她开始把那些苔藓往外拉。三四只蜜蜂"嗡嗡嗡嗡"地飞了出来。"这简直是非法入侵！"点点鼠夫人叫起来，"我要把他们赶出去——可是，谁能帮我呢？"她的脑海里闪过邻居蛤蟆杰克逊先生的身影。"不

行，他住在树篱下又脏又潮湿的排水沟里，脚总是脏兮兮的，会把地板弄脏。

10

tā jué dìng chī le wǎn cān hòu zài qù gǎn zǒu
她决定吃了晚餐后再去赶走

nà xiē mì fēng　　dāng huí dào kè tīng shí　　tā kàn dào
那些蜜蜂。当回到客厅时，她看到

jié kè xùn xiān sheng zhèng zuò zài nà lǐ　　tā pàng pàng de shēn tǐ jǐ zài yì zhāng
杰克逊先生正坐在那里！他胖胖的身体挤在一张

xiǎo yáo yǐ li　　liǎng zhī jiǎo jià zài bì lú de wéi lán shang
小摇椅里，两只脚架在壁炉的围栏上！

nín hái hǎo ba
"您还好吧，

jié kè xùn xiān sheng tiān
杰克逊先生？天

na nín shī tòu le
哪，您湿透了！"

xiè xie xiè xie xiè
"谢谢，谢谢，谢

xie diǎn diǎn shǔ fū rén
谢，点点鼠夫人！

wǒ zuò yí huì er bǎ zì
我坐一会儿，把自

jǐ hōng gān tā shuō tā zuò zài nà lǐ wēi xiào zhe shuǐ cóng tā de wài
己烘干。"他说。他坐在那里微笑着，水从他的外

tào xià bǎi dī dào dì bǎn shang diǎn diǎn shǔ fū rén zhǐ hǎo yòng tuō bǎ bù tíng
套下摆滴到地板上。点点鼠夫人只好用拖把不停

de tuō lái tuō qù
地拖来拖去。

jié kè xùn xiān sheng zuò le hěn jiǔ diǎn diǎn shǔ fū rén zhǐ hǎo wèn tā
杰克逊先生坐了很久,点点鼠夫人只好问他

yào bú yào yì qǐ chī wǎn cān tā duān lái le yīng táo hé xiè xie xiè
要不要一起吃晚餐。她端来了樱桃核。"谢谢,谢

xie diǎn diǎn shǔ fū rén wǒ méi yǒu yá chǐ méi yǒu yá chǐ jié kè
谢,点点鼠夫人!我没有牙齿,没有牙齿!"杰克

xùn xiān sheng shuō tā bǎ zuǐ zhāng de dà dà de tā zuǐ li què shí yì kē
逊先生说。他把嘴张得大大的,他嘴里确实一颗

yá chǐ yě méi yǒu
牙齿也没有!

13

点点鼠夫人又端来了蓟花种子。杰克逊先生却打起了喷嚏，"阿嚏，阿嚏！噗！"他喷得蓟花毛满屋子飞，"谢谢，谢谢！可我真正想吃的是一碟蜂蜜！"点点鼠夫人说："我恐怕满足不了您！"杰克逊先生微笑着说："我闻到您家里有蜂蜜的味道，所以才会来拜访您啊！"

<ruby>杰<rt>jié</rt></ruby><ruby>克<rt>kè</rt></ruby><ruby>逊<rt>xùn</rt></ruby><ruby>先<rt>xiān</rt></ruby><ruby>生<rt>sheng</rt></ruby><ruby>笨<rt>bèn</rt></ruby><ruby>手<rt>shǒu</rt></ruby><ruby>笨<rt>bèn</rt></ruby><ruby>脚<rt>jiǎo</rt></ruby><ruby>地<rt>de</rt></ruby><ruby>站<rt>zhàn</rt></ruby><ruby>起<rt>qǐ</rt></ruby><ruby>来<rt>lái</rt></ruby>，<ruby>开<rt>kāi</rt></ruby><ruby>始<rt>shǐ</rt></ruby><ruby>察<rt>chá</rt></ruby><ruby>看<rt>kàn</rt></ruby><ruby>点<rt>diǎn</rt></ruby><ruby>点<rt>diǎn</rt></ruby><ruby>鼠<rt>shǔ</rt></ruby><ruby>夫<rt>fū</rt></ruby><ruby>人<rt>rén</rt></ruby><ruby>的<rt>de</rt></ruby><ruby>食<rt>shí</rt></ruby><ruby>品<rt>pǐn</rt></ruby><ruby>柜<rt>guì</rt></ruby>。<ruby>点<rt>diǎn</rt></ruby><ruby>点<rt>diǎn</rt></ruby><ruby>鼠<rt>shǔ</rt></ruby><ruby>夫<rt>fū</rt></ruby><ruby>人<rt>rén</rt></ruby><ruby>拿<rt>ná</rt></ruby><ruby>着<rt>zhe</rt></ruby><ruby>一<rt>yí</rt></ruby><ruby>块<rt>kuài</rt></ruby><ruby>抹<rt>mā</rt></ruby><ruby>布<rt>bù</rt></ruby><ruby>跟<rt>gēn</rt></ruby><ruby>在<rt>zài</rt></ruby><ruby>他<rt>tā</rt></ruby><ruby>身<rt>shēn</rt></ruby><ruby>后<rt>hòu</rt></ruby>，<ruby>不<rt>bù</rt></ruby><ruby>停<rt>tíng</rt></ruby><ruby>地<rt>de</rt></ruby><ruby>擦<rt>cā</rt></ruby><ruby>着<rt>zhe</rt></ruby><ruby>他<rt>tā</rt></ruby><ruby>在<rt>zài</rt></ruby><ruby>客<rt>kè</rt></ruby><ruby>厅<rt>tīng</rt></ruby><ruby>地<rt>dì</rt></ruby><ruby>板<rt>bǎn</rt></ruby><ruby>上<rt>shang</rt></ruby><ruby>留<rt>liú</rt></ruby><ruby>下<rt>xià</rt></ruby><ruby>的<rt>de</rt></ruby><ruby>那<rt>nà</rt></ruby><ruby>些<rt>xiē</rt></ruby><ruby>巨<rt>jù</rt></ruby><ruby>大<rt>dà</rt></ruby><ruby>的<rt>de</rt></ruby><ruby>湿<rt>shī</rt></ruby><ruby>脚<rt>jiǎo</rt></ruby><ruby>印<rt>yìn</rt></ruby>。

食品柜里的确没有蜂蜜，于是，杰克逊先生又沿着走道向前走去。点点鼠夫人赶紧跟上去说："您挤不进去的，真的，真的，杰克逊先生！"杰克逊先生还是打着喷嚏挤进了餐具室。

他边找边问："阿嚏，阿嚏，阿嚏！这里也没有蜂蜜吗，点点鼠夫人？"三只小爬虫正躲在餐具架上。杰克逊先生一把抓住了最小的一只爬虫，另外两只赶紧逃走了。

然后他挤进了食品室。一只正在那里偷吃方糖的蝴蝶立即飞到窗外去了。杰克逊先生说："点点鼠夫人，看来您的客人不少啊！"点点鼠夫人生气地回答："全都是不请自来的！"他们沿着沙土走道向前走去。

17

"阿嚏——""嗡嗡！嗡嗡！"杰克逊先生在拐角遇到了那只大黄蜂，他一把抓住她，马上又把她放下了。"我不喜欢全身竖着毛的黄蜂！"杰克逊先生说着，用他的袖子擦了擦嘴。大黄蜂尖叫道："出去，你这只肮脏的癞蛤蟆！"

杰克逊先生在一间储藏室里找到了一个蜂巢，他想把它拉出来，点点鼠夫人赶紧躲进了坚果储藏室里。

当她走出储藏室时，客人们都已经走了。可到处都脏兮兮的：滴下的蜂蜜、苔藓、蓟花毛，还有大大小小的脏脚印！点点鼠夫人快发疯了！

她把家里清理了一下，然后，出去找了些嫩树枝，围住了门口："我把门口弄得这么小，杰克逊先生就进不来了！"

她想把家里打扫干净。可她累得什么也做不了了，于是坐在椅子上打起了瞌睡，嘴里还说着："什么时候才能像从前那样整洁呢？"

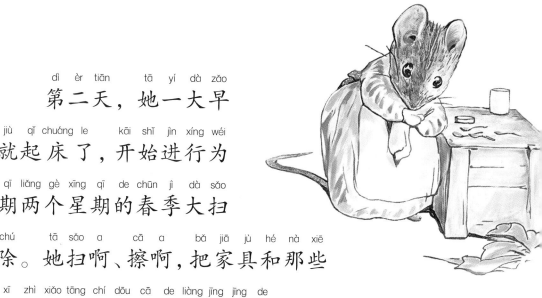

dì èr tiān　　tā yí dà zǎo
第二天，她一大早

jiù qǐ chuáng le　　kāi shǐ jìn xíng wéi
就起床了，开始进行为

qī liǎng gè xīng qī de chūn jì dà sǎo
期两个星期的春季大扫

chú　　tā sǎo a　　cā a　　bǎ jiā jù hé nà xiē
除。她扫啊、擦啊，把家具和那些

xī zhì xiǎo tāng chí dōu cā de liàng jīng jīng de
锡质小汤匙都擦得亮晶晶的。

dāng jiā li biàn de yòu gān jìng yòu piào liang shí　　tā jǔ bàn le　　yì chǎng
当家里变得又干净又漂亮时，她举办了一场

yàn huì　　kè rén shì wǔ zhī xiǎo lǎo shǔ　　méi yǒu jié kè xùn xiān sheng　　jié kè
宴会，客人是五只小老鼠，没有杰克逊先生。杰克

xùn xiān sheng yì wén dào yàn huì shang de xiāng qì
逊先生一闻到宴会上的香气，

jiù shàng le àn　　kě shì tā wú fǎ cóng diǎn diǎn
就上了岸，可是他无法从点点

shǔ fū rén jiā de mén jǐ jìn qù
鼠夫人家的门挤进去。

于是，小老鼠们从窗口递给杰克逊先生满满一橡子杯蜂蜜。杰克逊先生一点儿也没有生气。

他在外面，坐在阳光下，还说："阿嚏，阿嚏，阿嚏！祝您身体健康，点点鼠夫人！"

22

弗洛浦茜家的小兔子

yǒu rén shuō　　chī tài duō wō jù huì fàn kùn　　wǒ cóng méi zài chī guo
有人说，吃太多莴苣会犯困。我从没在吃过

wō jù hòu dǎ kē shuì　　kě shì　　duì fú luò pǔ xī jiā de xiǎo tù zi men
莴苣后打瞌睡。可是，对弗洛浦茜家的小兔子们

lái shuō　　wō jù dí què jù yǒu hěn qiáng de cuī mián gōng néng
来说，莴苣的确具有很强的催眠功能。

23

xiǎo tù zi běn jié míngzhǎng dà hòu　　hé biǎo mèi fú luò pǔ xī
小兔子本杰明长大后，和表妹弗洛浦茜

jié le hūn　　yīn wèi tā men de bǎo bao hěn duō　　suǒ yǐ zhè xiē tù
结了婚。因为他们的宝宝很多，所以这些兔

bǎo bao tōng cháng dōu bèi
宝宝通常都被

jiào zuò　　fú luò pǔ xī
叫作"弗洛浦茜

jiā de xiǎo tù zi
家的小兔子"。

对这一大家子来说，食物并不总是够吃的——

本杰明就会从弗洛浦茜的弟弟那儿借几棵卷心菜。

弗洛浦茜的弟弟就是小兔子彼得，他自己有一个

菜园。

yǒu shí　　bǐ dé yě méi yǒu duō yú
有时,彼得也没有多余

de juǎn xīn cài jiè gěi tā men
的卷心菜借给他们。

zhè shí hou　　fú luò pǔ xī jiā de
这时候,弗洛浦茜家的

xiǎo tù zi men jiù huì chuān guò tián yě　　dào
小兔子们就会穿过田野,到

yí gè fèi wù duī li zhǎo chī de　　zhè ge
一个废物堆里找吃的。这个

fèi wù duī jiù zài mài kè xiān sheng jiā cài yuán
废物堆就在麦克先生家菜园

wài de gōu qú li
外的沟渠里。

26

麦克先生的废物堆里什么都有——果酱瓶、纸袋，还有割草机割下的一堆堆青草，那些青草摸起来滑溜溜的。有一天，那里居然有一些很老的莴苣，甚至还开了花。小兔子们开心极了。

小兔子们毫不犹豫地大嚼起莴苣来，肚子都撑得圆鼓鼓的。不一会儿，他们就犯困了，一个个都倒在割下的青草上。本杰明进入梦乡前，在自己的头上套了一个纸袋，以防备那些讨厌的苍蝇。

<ruby>弗<rt>fú</rt></ruby><ruby>洛<rt>luò</rt></ruby><ruby>浦<rt>pǔ</rt></ruby><ruby>茜<rt>xī</rt></ruby><ruby>家<rt>jiā</rt></ruby>
<ruby>的<rt>de</rt></ruby><ruby>小<rt>xiǎo</rt></ruby><ruby>兔<rt>tù</rt></ruby><ruby>子<rt>zi</rt></ruby><ruby>们<rt>men</rt></ruby><ruby>在<rt>zài</rt></ruby><ruby>暖<rt>nuǎn</rt></ruby>
<ruby>暖<rt>nuǎn</rt></ruby><ruby>的<rt>de</rt></ruby><ruby>阳<rt>yáng</rt></ruby><ruby>光<rt>guāng</rt></ruby><ruby>下<rt>xia</rt></ruby><ruby>美<rt>měi</rt></ruby><ruby>美<rt>měi</rt></ruby>
<ruby>地<rt>de</rt></ruby><ruby>睡<rt>shuì</rt></ruby><ruby>着<rt>zhe</rt></ruby>。<ruby>苍<rt>cāng</rt></ruby><ruby>蝇<rt>ying</rt></ruby><ruby>们<rt>men</rt></ruby>

<ruby>"嗡<rt>wēng</rt></ruby><ruby>嗡<rt>wēng</rt></ruby><ruby>嗡"<rt>wēng</rt></ruby><ruby>地<rt>de</rt></ruby><ruby>绕<rt>rào</rt></ruby><ruby>着<rt>zhe</rt></ruby><ruby>围<rt>wéi</rt></ruby><ruby>墙<rt>qiáng</rt></ruby><ruby>吵<rt>chǎo</rt></ruby><ruby>个<rt>gè</rt></ruby><ruby>不<rt>bù</rt></ruby><ruby>停<rt>tíng</rt></ruby>，<ruby>还<rt>hái</rt></ruby><ruby>有<rt>yǒu</rt></ruby><ruby>一<rt>yì</rt></ruby><ruby>只<rt>zhī</rt></ruby><ruby>小<rt>xiǎo</rt></ruby><ruby>老<rt>lǎo</rt></ruby><ruby>鼠<rt>shǔ</rt></ruby>
<ruby>正<rt>zhèng</rt></ruby><ruby>在<rt>zài</rt></ruby><ruby>废<rt>fèi</rt></ruby><ruby>物<rt>wù</rt></ruby><ruby>堆<rt>duī</rt></ruby><ruby>的<rt>de</rt></ruby><ruby>果<rt>guǒ</rt></ruby><ruby>酱<rt>jiàng</rt></ruby><ruby>瓶<rt>píng</rt></ruby><ruby>里<rt>li</rt></ruby><ruby>找<rt>zhǎo</rt></ruby><ruby>吃<rt>chī</rt></ruby><ruby>的<rt>de</rt></ruby>。<ruby>这<rt>zhè</rt></ruby><ruby>是<rt>shì</rt></ruby><ruby>一<rt>yì</rt></ruby><ruby>只<rt>zhī</rt></ruby><ruby>长<rt>cháng</rt></ruby><ruby>尾<rt>wěi</rt></ruby><ruby>巴<rt>ba</rt></ruby>
<ruby>丛<rt>cóng</rt></ruby><ruby>林<rt>lín</rt></ruby><ruby>鼠<rt>shǔ</rt></ruby>，<ruby>她<rt>tā</rt></ruby><ruby>就<rt>jiù</rt></ruby><ruby>是<rt>shì</rt></ruby><ruby>点<rt>diǎn</rt></ruby><ruby>点<rt>diǎn</rt></ruby><ruby>鼠<rt>shǔ</rt></ruby><ruby>夫<rt>fū</rt></ruby><ruby>人<rt>rén</rt></ruby>。

点点鼠夫人"沙沙沙"地爬过纸袋，把本杰明吵醒了。点点鼠夫人和本杰明 正在谈话，头顶突然传来一阵重 重的脚步声。

接着，一整袋刚割下的青草倒在了熟睡的小兔子们身上，是麦克先生！本杰明赶紧躲到纸袋下，点点鼠夫人也钻进了果酱瓶。

xiǎo tù zi men zài zhè yí zhèn cǎo yǔ xia réng rán tián tián de shuì
小兔子们在这一阵"草雨"下仍然甜甜地睡

zhe tā men mèng jiàn mā ma zhèng zài bāng tā men zhěng lǐ gān cǎo chuáng ne mài
着,他们梦见妈妈正在帮他们整理干草床呢！麦

kè xiān sheng dào kōng cǎo dài hòu xiàng xià kàn le kàn tā kàn jiàn qīng cǎo li huá
克先生倒空草袋后向下看了看。他看见青草里滑

jī de shù zhe jǐ zhī xiǎo ěr duo
稽地竖着几只小耳朵！

mài kè xiān sheng zǒu le guò lái
麦克先生走了过来——

yī èr sān sì wǔ liù zhī xiǎo
"一、二、三、四、五……六只小

tù zi tā biān shǔ zhe biān jiāng xiǎo tù zi
兔子!"他边数着边将小兔子

men zhuāng jìn le tā de cǎo dài
们装进了他的草袋。

xiǎo tù zi men zhè shí mèng jiàn mā ma
小兔子们这时梦见妈妈

gěi tā men fān le gè shēn tā men zài shuì mèng zhōng niǔ le niǔ shēn zi kě
给他们翻了个身!他们在睡梦中扭了扭身子,可

shì hái méi xǐng lái mài kè xiān sheng bǎ
是还没醒来。麦克先生把

dài zi zā jǐn hòu fàng dào wéi qiáng shang
袋子扎紧后放到围墙上

le tā yòu zǒu dào cǎo píng nà er
了。他又走到草坪那儿,

zhǔn bèi shōu qǐ gē cǎo jī
准备收起割草机。

麦克先生走了之后，原本留在家里的兔妈妈
弗洛浦茜穿过田野，向这里走来。她疑惑地看着
围墙上的那只口袋，想知道她的小兔子们都到哪
儿去了。

这时，点点鼠夫人跑出了果酱瓶，本杰明也拿开了他头上的纸袋，他们向弗洛浦茜讲述了刚刚发生的悲剧。本杰明和弗洛浦茜简直绝望了，他们解不开口袋上的绳子。但足智多谋的点点鼠夫人在口袋下面咬出了一个洞。小兔子们都被拉出来拍醒了。他们的父母把三个烂西葫芦、一把旧毛刷和两个烂萝卜塞进了空口袋里。

然后，他们全都

藏进矮树丛里，等着

麦克先生过来。

麦克先生回来后，

拿起那只口袋就走。他

吃力地提着口袋，看来那

只口袋相当重呢！弗洛

浦茜家的小兔子们在安

全距离外远远地跟着他。

tā men kàn zhe mài kè xiān sheng zǒu
他们看着麦克先生走
jìn le tā de fáng zi　rán hòu niè shǒu niè
进了他的房子，然后蹑手蹑
jiǎo de pá dào chuāng kǒu xia　xiǎng tīng ting wū
脚地爬到窗口下，想听听屋
li　de dòng jing
里的动静。

mài kè xiān sheng jiāng kǒu dai rēng zài shí
麦克先生将口袋扔在石
dì bǎn shang　rú guǒ xiǎo tù zi men hái zài
地板上。如果小兔子们还在
kǒu dai li　kěn dìng huì bèi shuāi de hěn téng　tā
口袋里，肯定会被摔得很疼。他
men tīng dào mài kè xiān sheng lā guò lái yì bǎ yǐ
们听到麦克先生拉过来一把椅
zi　gē gē gē　de xiào le qǐ lái　yī
子，"咯咯咯"地笑了起来。"一、
èr sān sì wǔ　　liù zhī xiǎo tù zi
二、三、四、五……六只小兔子！"
tā lè huài le
他乐坏了！

"咦，那是什么东西？"麦克太太问道。"六只肥肥的小兔子！"麦克先生回答。

那只最小的兔子在这时爬上了窗台。麦克太太提起口袋摸了摸："我可以用兔皮做斗篷。"

"做斗篷？"麦克先生叫道，"我要卖了他们买烟草！""我要剥下他们的皮，砍下他们的头！"

mài kè tài tai bǎ kǒu dai jiě kāi　　jiāng shǒu shēn le jìn qù　　dāng tā

麦克太太把口袋解开，将手伸了进去。当她

fā xiàn kǒu dai li zhǐ yǒu yì xiē làn shū cài shí　　tā fèn nù de pò kǒu dà

发现口袋里只有一些烂蔬菜时，她愤怒地破口大

mà　shuō mài kè xiān sheng jiǎn zhí shì　　jū xīn bù liáng

骂，说麦克先生简直是"居心不良"。

麦克先生也非
常气愤。一个烂西葫
芦飞出厨房的窗口，
打中了那只最小的兔
子。真疼！

这时，本杰明和
弗洛浦茜想着他们该
回家了。

麦克先生没有得到他的烟草，麦克太太也没有得到她的兔皮。倒是点点鼠夫人，在圣诞节收到了一大包兔毛，完全够她给自己织一件斗篷、一条头巾、一只漂亮的暖手笼和一副温暖的连指手套了！